M W
& R

A Fool in Paradise

A FOOL IN PARADISE

An Artist's Early Life

Doris McCarthy

MACFARLANE WALTER & ROSS
TORONTO

First edition

Macfarlane Walter & Ross
550 Queen Street East
Toronto, Canada M5A 1V2

CANADIAN CATALOGUING IN PUBLICATION DATA

McCarthy, Doris, 1910-
    A fool in paradise: an artist's early life

Includes bibliographical references.
ISBN 0-921912-03-X

1. McCarthy, Doris, 1910-   . 2. Women painters -
Canada - Biography.   3. Landscape painters -
Canada - Biography.   I. Title.

ND249.M33A2 1990   759.11   C90-093381-X

"Domestic Bliss, Fool's Paradise II, 1948"
by Doris McCarthy courtesy of
The Wynick/Tuck Gallery, Toronto, Ontario

Printed and bound in Canada

To you my friends, whether teachers, students, Shawnees, neighbours, or chance acquaintances, whose names do not appear in this book but whom I love, and who will know that it was only because there was not enough room that you are not here by name, I dedicate this fragment of the life that you helped me live.

Contents

Acknowledgements

THIS IS THE STORY of my becoming, of the years and the people who made me the person I am. This book holds the first half of my life, from my birth to my fortieth year, when the formative influences had done their most important work. Its writing began as an assignment in a creative writing course at Scarborough College with Professor Russell Brown, and it developed during a second year of creative writing under the supervision of Professor Alan Thomas. With the encouragement of these professors I explored my life, discovering its shape, and under the guidance of my editor and publisher Jan Walter I have been able to prepare this first part for publication. To these three I offer my appreciative thanks. Each of them was a critical but perceptive reader. What more could any writer ask? More, however, was given in the form of practical help in bringing the writing to the attention of a publisher by my neighbour and friend Barbara Moon, and by Jack McClelland, whom I approached on her advice and who consented to act as my agent.

For these weeks and months of enjoyment in discovering myself, I thank them all.

1948 Domestic Bliss Fools Paradise II 1/40   Doris McCarthy

1

First Light

I WAS BROUGHT UP on the nursery rhyme about Monday's child and Tuesday's child, and since I was a Thursday's child I took it for received truth that I would have "far to go" and do a lot of travelling in my life. The family had moved about a great deal even before I was born because my father, George Arnold McCarthy, was a civil engineer who was sent by the construction company that employed him to wherever the project was located. He married Mary Jane Colson Moffatt – Jennie for short – in Montreal in 1901, and they went to live in Niagara Falls, where he was assistant chief engineer for the building of its first big hydroelectric plant. My eldest brother, Kenneth, was born there. Mother was hardly more than a bride, inexperienced at housekeeping, ignorant about babies, and with no family or hired girl to help her. She made all her mistakes on Kenneth.

Five years later they were in North Bay, where Dad

was in charge of the extension of the railroad north to Timmins, and there my brother Douglas was born. He was a perfect baby, all round and rosy with a smile for everyone. Mother adored him. No wonder poor little Kenny started being naughty and telling lies. Nobody knew about replacement trauma in those days and Mother marched Kenneth off to the local minister for moral instruction.

By the time I arrived, in 1910, the family was living in Calgary, and Florence Hicks, a wonderful young Cornish woman, had been taken on as domestic help. I was blessed in being a girl after two boys and in having three adults to love me and make me welcome. Mother used to enjoy telling about her first sight of me, my head covered with dark hair, which the nurses had put into little braids tied at the end with coloured ribbons. She wondered if they had given her an Indian baby by mistake.

My own earliest memory is of fluffy yellow chicks running about behind wire netting, their thin legs like the wire ones on toy chicks that could be bent this way or that to make them stand up. Mother said the real chicks that I remember were at Mr. Cousins's farm outside Vancouver, where we were living the summer I turned two. And from that same summer I remember gulls, clean white shapes against the blue sky, almost motionless in the air as they floated behind the ferry, their heads turning from side to side watching for the scraps of bread Kenneth was throwing. My first memories are full of sunshine.

But my next is sombre. When my father was transferred again, Mother was dismayed. She loved Vancouver and wanted to stay in the house Dad had bought there, but not without him. They decided to leave house

and furniture to tenants and make do with rented accommodation for the new job in Boise, Idaho, so that it was
in an apartment-hotel in Boise that we spent the Christmas of 1912 and I had my first remembered experience
of sorrow. The little girl in the suite next to us broke the
doll that Santa Claus had brought me that morning. I can
still see the dark pattern of the wallpaper in the dusky
corridor that I ran along, screaming, to reach Mother and
comfort.

Sometime during the next summer, after we had
moved once again, to a construction project in California,
my father's employers went bankrupt, ending the American interlude but not our travelling. When Dad found
himself out of a job he took us east to the old family home
in Moncton, New Brunswick, to see Grandfather Mc-
Carthy, who was gravely ill. Grandfather was a patriarch
in fact and in appearance, erect and handsome, with a
flowing beard. His father had come out from Ireland early
in the nineteenth century and married a woman whose
family was already two generations Canadian. Great-
grandfather McCarthy had been a wheelwright and a
Roman Catholic, but he apprenticed his son to a Protestant, and Grandfather became a Presbyterian and eventually a qualified naval blacksmith.

The austere two-storey frame house where he lay ill
was familiar to us from a photograph that had hung on
the wall wherever we went. But the big Lombardy pop-
lars in the picture were gone, cut off at shoulder height.
While we were visiting in Moncton Dad took a snapshot
of one of them with Dougie and me sitting on top, our
legs dangling, two chubby children squinting into the sun,
and Kenneth, eleven years old now and growing tall,

standing behind us. I suspect that we three lived not at
the old King Street home behind the poplar stumps but
at Aunt Adelaide's much larger house on the hill. Her
husband, Uncle Matthew Lodge, was a stout, bluff, ex-
pansive sort of man, whose later visits to us were notable
for the new doll he always brought for me and the
pervasive smell of cigar smoke that lingered the next day.

I was too young at that time to realize all the implications of the Moncton visit. Dad's mother had been an
invalid after his birth and had died many years earlier.
His strongest bonds were with his father and his eldest
sister, Molly, who had brought him up and encouraged
him to go to university. He now was faced with considering anew how best to meet the responsibility of providing
for his wife and three children. He must have been
conscious of the strain on Mother of the constant moves,
and of how they had disrupted Kenneth's education.
Douglas had turned six and was ready to start school.
Before we left Moncton Dad had decided to forgo the
tempting fees offered to a free-lance engineer and to settle
for the security and stability of a government job. By the
fall of 1913 he was a city engineer with the works department in Toronto, in charge of railways and bridges, and
we were living in a rented red brick house on Sherbourne
Street a block or so north of Allan Gardens. He could
walk to his office in the City Hall.

Toronto was a small city in those days, conservative,
sedate, known as a "city of churches" and very British.
Eaton's and Simpson's were institutions central to the
lives of its citizens, two big department stores facing each
other across the busiest intersection in the city. Eaton's
was the larger and more popular, home to generations of

Toronto shoppers before the motor car and suburban malls changed the pattern of retail business. Simpson's was directed more to the carriage trade with its slogan "You'll *enjoy* shopping at Simpson's." The McCarthys didn't think of themselves as carriage trade. (When Mother and Dad were looking for a Toronto home, they were interested in a house in Rosedale until someone warned them that if you lived in Rosedale you couldn't be seen on a ladder washing your own windows.) We were an Eaton's family. Dad teased Mother by telling her that on pay-day he took his cheque from the City Hall and walked across the street to put it in his Eaton's deposit account. Eaton's had grown on a policy of no credit; in those days you put the money in first and then shopped with it.

The morning parade of Eaton's delivery wagons was one of the sights of Toronto, each red and blue wagon pulled by a matched pair of dappled grey-and-white horses. They trotted up Bay Street in smooth sequence until the ones bound for the east and west turned off and went their separate ways. The delivery man on our route became a friend, calling two or three times a week with staple groceries and all our other household needs, carrying in the parcels without waiting to be admitted, knowing everyone's name. One cold dark morning in November, to my delight but to Mother's chagrin, the Eaton's man brought a shiny scarlet doll's sleigh through the front door of the house on Sherbourne Street. I accepted Mother's hasty explanation that it had come to our address by mistake, and I have forgotten what I thought when it reappeared on Christmas morning.

My father was not really a city man. He loved the

outdoors and the water and wanted to be closer to the
lake. Summer of 1914 saw us about ten miles west of
Toronto in a cottage at Long Branch, then a summer
resort on Lake Ontario. There was a lively social life
among the wives and children during the day, and a
reliable train service so that all the husbands who worked
in the city could get home in time for dinner at night.

Now the memories crowd. Early in the morning Dad
would be over in the dew-wet grass of the bowling green
across the road, picking mushrooms, which Florrie
cooked with the bacon for breakfast. The whole family
went swimming together on Sunday morning because
Dad was home that day. (Saturday morning was work as
usual for everyone back then.) I was a fairy at the summer
residents' masquerade, dressed in a stiff tutu of pink
tarlatan with wings held in shape by a wire frame. Mother
and Florrie sewed sequins all over me to make me sparkle.
Helen Halford was a matching blue fairy. The Halfords
lived in a cottage nearby, Helen and her mother and a
brother who was about Doug's age, but it is Mr. Halford
whom I remember best. When the families were visiting
together he would make faces, indescribably grotesque
and funny, to send us into helpless laughter. When summer was over and both families were back in Toronto, I
was allowed to make a telephone call, my first-ever, to
him.

Florrie was part of the family. It was she who filled the
round galvanized-iron tub with water for the Saturday-
night bath that I shared with Dougie. She read us the
"Uncle Wiggley" stories that appeared every night in the
Evening Telegram, which Dad carried home with him on
the train. Uncle Wiggley was a rabbit who had remark-

able adventures. Was it Dad or Uncle Wiggley that I was waiting for the day I disappeared from the house and was found sitting on the railway track?

Doug tells me that there was a rope swing hung from the big tree in the vacant lot beside the cottage and that Ken used to swing on it higher than anyone else. And it was that summer that I found Mother downstairs in the sitting room having tea with other ladies when I needed to have her pull my panties up after I had successfully gone to the toilet all by myself.

I remember especially a spectacular thunderstorm one night, with lightning snaking down over the lake and cracks of thunder to shake the cottage. My father took me in his arms out onto the veranda and watched it with me, holding me tight and secure. I have not been afraid of storms since that day. Dad was a quiet man, not comic like Mr. Halford nor deep-voiced and important-looking like Uncle Matthew. Mother was the one who did all the talking, but Dad was the rock, the strength, the refuge.

It was while we were in Long Branch that Dougie came home waving a newspaper and calling out that war had been declared. I must have had some sense of what that meant, perhaps from the way Florrie and Mother reacted to the news. It was not long before grown-ups talked of very little else and every family had someone, or had neighbours with someone, who had joined up. I have a vivid picture of the breakfast table at Balsam Avenue a few years later. Breakfast was a formal meal with all five of us at the table and Florrie serving. Dad would shake out his morning paper to find the right page and look up the casualty list. "There's a Jarvis here, Jenny, killed in action: Donald Bruce. Could that be

Bert's youngest?" "Missing" was a separate heading, and
"Wounded" seemed almost like good news after that.

In 1913 "the Beach," a summer resort on Lake Ontario
just east of Toronto, was taken into the city and became
a permissible place for a civic employee to live. R.C.
Harris, commissioner of works and Dad's boss, built
himself a fine new house close to the lake on newly
opened-up Munro Park Boulevard. By the time the Long
Branch summer was over Dad had found a house to rent
on Maclean Avenue just above Queen Street. Queen
Street was the one paved road that ran parallel to the lake
right across the city. Side-streets at the Beach were sandy
and apt to trap the few motor cars. The streetcars came
east on Queen Street as far as Maclean Avenue and
turned there. From Queen Street down to the lake,
Maclean Avenue bordered the woods of Scarborough
Beach Park, which lay between it and the city. Above
Queen, Maclean continued north beside a ravine that cut
through the bush up to Kingston Road, the main highway
(still unpaved) to the distant town of Kingston. The
ravine was punctuated with three ponds, the largest down
near Queen, where it emptied into a culvert that ran
under the street. We learned to skate on those ponds, but
it was in beautiful Lake Ontario with its fine pebble and
sand beach that we all went bathing and learned to swim.
    The family lived on Maclean for the first three years of
the war, long enough to confuse my sequence of memories. To know right hand from left I must stand again
facing the kitchen window. My right is the one on the
same side as the backyard. North is the house where the

Arnolds lived. Mary Arnold was the little girl whose doll
I stole, earning me the only serious spanking I remember.
There was a second instalment to that spanking when I
was discovered to have lightened my banishment to
Mother's bedroom by using her nail scissors to cut off the
bristles of her best silver-backed hairbrush.

Still, the happy times were legion. Birthdays took us
down to Scarborough Beach Park, a wonderful place
with picnic tables beside the long sandy beach, and a
whole amusement park between Queen Street and the
lake. There was a miniature train, a real steam engine
pulling a string of cars behind it, each an open carriage
with seats for four. It carried passengers on a twisting
course through the woods that ran along the west side of
lower Maclean, and then out of the woods and past some
of the booths where people fired guns or threw balls to
win kewpie dolls. The Shoot-the-Chutes was a perilous
ride in a boat winched up by chain to a tower, where it
paused, trembling, above the slide that would plunge it
with a great splash into the pool at the bottom amid
squeals of fright and excitement. More accessible, because it was free, was the Bump-the-Bumps, a wide slide
of polished wood swelling here and there into smooth
rounded hillocks that swung you off course and sometimes turned you completely about so that you arrived
facing backwards. When we had played on the Bump-
the-Bumps long enough, we went down to the table
beside the lake where Mother and Florrie were putting
out plates and unpacking sandwiches, ready for Dad's
arrival after work. The birthday cake was a triumphant
climax, a big round layer cake, iced alternately pink and
chocolate between ruchings of icing and with the right

number of candles. Becoming a year older meant something in those days.

Up the street lived Freddie Hood with his older sister,
Barbara, and their mother and father. Freddie was almost
my age and became my playmate. Together we explored
the woods behind his house, finding mossy stumps that
were obviously fairy palaces. Freddie's father was good
with children and showed us new games. Easter morning
brought ashy rabbit tracks to the living-room carpet, and
following them led to hidden treasures of jelly beans and
even chocolate Easter eggs. Mr. Hood had made a long
bobsleigh, able to take ten of us at once, and many a
winter Saturday afternoon was spent dragging it up the
steep path through the woods to the top of Pine Crescent
and careening down the long S curve and up the sharp
slope at the bottom to the head of Maclean Avenue with
Mr. Hood at the helm. Kenneth was eight years older than
I and beyond most of the things that Dougie and I shared,
but even Ken joined in that fun.

And we all skated on the ponds. There was the day that
Ken was skating backwards towards the overflow that
carried the stream under Queen Street, when he fell in
and disappeared. The other children gathered at the edge
of the drain, but all they could see was the water flowing
down into darkness. Two of them carried Ken's boots
home to Mother. When he turned up wet at the house,
stumbling in his skates, and explaining that he had
crawled through the culvert under the street and come
out into the gully on the other side, Mother's terror
exploded into angry tears, and it was weeks before any
of us was allowed on the ice again.

Spring was when the gutters began to run melt-water

and the boys brought out marbles, pee-wees no bigger than peas, regular marbles the size of cherries, and larger glass allies with streaks and swirls of colour fused mysteriously into them. Girls took to skipping-ropes, lengths of heavy cord from somebody's cellar or real store ropes with painted wooden handles.

My birthday came in July, allowing me to start kindergarten as soon as I had turned five. Freddie was too young to go with me but Barbara Hood made a dependable escort to get me there safely. However, kindergarten children were dismissed earlier than the big girls. There was some wretched little boy released at the same time as I who discovered the fun of chasing me. I was a chubby little girl, not built for speed. For a few afternoons he terrorized me, until Mother found out and arranged for me to be given a five-minute head start. I ran all the way home to protect my lead. I wonder if, as Mother predicted, he came to a Bad End.

One early memory from Maclean Avenue is of the day my father went back to the cottage at Long Branch to paddle the canoe home to the Beach. It was an autumn morning, cold and miserable, with a mean wind. Mother was very anxious because the lake was rough and he was alone. Since I was too young to leave she bundled me up and took me with her down to the lakeshore at the bottom of Maclean, where we stood like figures out of an old-fashioned melodrama, huddled together for warmth and comfort, straining our eyes to see above the waves. At first there was just a speck. But it grew, and became something real, and eventually recognizable. Mother never did get over her distrust of canoes but her children all learned to be at home in them.

Toronto had begun to grow before the war, but it was still concentrated south of the rising ground that was known simply as "the hill." Dad bought a piece of farmland on a country road that is now St. Clair Avenue just where Bathurst crosses it. Once a year Mother packed a picnic and we all, including Florrie, travelled by streetcar and then by radial car to this orchard, borrowed a ladder from the farmer, and picked our cherries. Dad's major project for the city at this time was building the Bloor Street Viaduct to take traffic across the Don Valley and allow Toronto to grow to the northeast.

One minor project, which he designed as well as built, was a pretty little bridge that spanned a waterway at Centre Island, close to where the ferry docked. Perhaps that is why we began to celebrate family birthdays at the Island. On one such day, before Dad had joined us, a small boy who had run away from his mother tripped and fell into the lagoon near our picnic table. He couldn't swim, and when Kenneth saw him flailing he jumped in to the rescue. Mother was alarmed, and then proud, as everyone declared Kenneth a hero, but his reward for heroism was the ordeal of travelling home by ferry and streetcar wrapped in Mother's ankle-length sweater to cover his nakedness.

Mother had her own embarrassing moment on the streetcar one day that same year, when my clear childish treble asked her if the Holy Ghost wore a white sheet. We three children all went to Sunday school at St. Aidan's Anglican Church on Queen Street at the Beach, until at five years of age I suddenly became a Presbyterian. On an especially important festival morning at St. Aidan's the

Sunday-school children were taken up into the church for part of their program. Lacking a hat, I was turned away at the door and sent home. Mother's response was to take me over to the nearest competition, Kew Beach Presbyterian Church, where, she assumed, the standards would be less ridiculous. However, the time came when I returned to St. Aidan's. The janitor at Kew Beach caught me stealing a sweet from the big tub of hard candies waiting to be put into Christmas stockings for the poor. I was ashamed ever to face him again, and made my own move back to join my brothers. This is my first public confession of the crime.

Even during the war the Beach was growing at a great pace. New houses were springing up, and Mother and Dad were looking for one. Sunday afternoons we went exploring the half-finished homes, climbing ladders to the second floor, comparing the floor plans, checking out the number of rooms. I did my own gleaning from the rubbish piles outside, finding beautiful ceramic insulators and small blocks of wood just right for furnishing my doll's house. In 1917 Mother and Dad settled on a house to buy. We were all around the dining-room table at a meal when they told us about it. "It's in the backyard of the big white house at the corner of Balsam and Pine," said Mother. "In the backyard?" I was appalled. I took my napkin ring to represent the yard, and put a crumb of bread in it. "You mean like that?" "Not quite," said my father.

Balsam Avenue was the next street east of Maclean. It bends at the top of the hill, just as Pine Avenue crosses it, and our new house, on land that once belonged to the big white house on the corner, faced down the steep hill and

commanded a view right to the lake. Whenever I turned
onto Balsam from Queen Street there was our front door
at the top of the hill saying "welcome home" to me. The
backyard was deep enough for a lawn with a family
garden swing, and beyond that a vegetable plot so that
we could do our bit for the war effort. There was a central
hall with the stairs going up to a landing with a triple
casement window. On the right of the hall was the living
room, twice the size of the one at Maclean Avenue or of
any other I remembered us having, with a real wood-
burning fireplace. A small porch opened out of it on the
street side, with a brick half-wall all around that made it
private. On the left of the front door was a dining room
quite equal to Mother's mahogany dining-room set,
which she had by this time retrieved from Vancouver.
The hall ran back past the stairs to the back door and the
kitchen with a roomy pantry between it and the dining
room. Upstairs Mother and Dad had the big bedroom
over the front door, their windows seeing over the trees
to the lake. I was next to them towards the back of the
house, close to Florrie's room, which looked down at the
backyard and the woods beyond. The two boys had the
bedroom on the street side with a sunroom from it over
the living-room porch. Next to their room, above the
front half of the living room, was the den with another
fireplace, which was our territory just as the living room
was Mother's, and we were free to play in it and entertain
our friends there. One bathroom served us all, demanding
a strict schedule of morning use. Across the fence the
neighbours on the north had a lot that ran through the
woods down into the ravine at the back all the way to the

third pond. Up in the tall oaks behind their house their
boys had a tree-loft, and those boys were of assorted ages
that matched our own family. What more could anyone
want?

Mother was a capable woman, well able to run a home
smoothly with Florrie's help, and with energy as well to
fling herself into all kinds of outside war work. She was
organizing tag days, singing with the Mendelssohn Choir
in benefit concerts, knitting "comforts for the boys," and
moving steadily up in the hierarchy of the Daughters of
the Empire, or IODE, as everyone called it. The most
eloquent comment on her outside work was made by our
talking parrot, who taught himself to mimic her many
telephone conversations. First a ring, two or three times,
then "Hello?" then "Hel-*lo*!" – pause – "Rub-a-gub, rub-
a-gub, rub-a-gub," long pause, "yes – yes," then the very
timbre of Mother's laughter, another pause, more rub-a-
gub, and eventually, "Well, good-bye," in Mother's own
lilt.

   She was a handsome woman, straight, somewhat
heavy ("Am I as fat as that woman, George?"), with
presence. When she walked across the room it was like
watching a ship in full sail. She had a strong sense of
drama. After my morning cuddle in bed with both my
parents, when Dad had vanished to the bathroom, she
would tell me fairy tales, and I would be there in the big
bed, watching her dress. Her long brown hair, after its
brushing, was divided into hanks, each one tied with a
shoe-lace, before being twisted up into a fashionable pile

on the top of her head. Meanwhile she was harrowing me
with the story of Bluebeard. Her voice wavered between
hope and terror. "Sister Anne – Sister Anne – is there
anyone coming?" This was my cue to burst into tears,
which I did every time. We both enjoyed our parts.

Mother had been a professional singer before she
married, soprano soloist at St. Andrew's Presbyterian
Church in Montreal. Dad fell in love with her voice when
he was a student at McGill, too poor to afford concert
tickets but able to walk to the big church on St. Catherine
Street and hear music for nothing. Mother herself was as
attractive as her voice, a beautiful girl and full of fun, but
nursing a bitter disappointment at being denied study
abroad. She had won a scholarship to study opera in
England but her parents wouldn't or couldn't let her use
it. A pity. Her voice was glorious, clear, true, and strong.
I can remember the sound of her soaring scales through
the closed door of the front parlour on Sherbourne Street.
When I was playing with the Hoods down on Maclean
Avenue, Mother could walk to the top of the path through
the woods to call me, and her voice carried the length of
a city block. Besides the voice, she had the temperament.
She made a stage of wherever she was. I think she looked
back wistfully all her life at the opportunity she had
missed, and I'm sure that was one of the reasons she
supported me in every effort I made to become an artist.

Mother's family had its roots in Quebec City, where
her great-grandmother had landed from Ireland, eighteen
years old, a "ward in Chancery." The story goes that she
arrived alone and terrified at the door of a lawyer's office
there, and fainted into the arms of the lawyer's clerk,
John Hunter, the man who would become her husband.

Her photograph at age eighty shows a strong Irish face, direct, confident. Of her twenty-one pregnancies only three children survived to maturity. Her one daughter, Mother's mother, married Grandpa Moffatt and moved eventually to Montreal, where Mother's brother, Dr. Charles Moffatt, became the leading heart specialist at the Royal Victoria Hospital. Grandfather's sisters were still in the old family home in Lévis, across the river from Quebec City, but Grandmother's brother, John Hunter, and his family had also moved up to Montreal.

The year that I was seven Mother took me to visit them all. Grandma's flat was a Victorian stage set, complete with antimacassars, upholstered chairs with silk swags and tassels, lace doilies, and wonderful arrangements of waxen flowers inside oval glass domes. On her dressing table was a pair of small silver horses pulling a carriage made of mother-of-pearl with silver wheels. On my dining-room table seventy years later is a silver butter dish with a silver cow lying on its lid that I first saw on her table in Montreal. Grandfather had a stereoscope, a marvellous peep-show that you held up to look through. There was a lens for each eye, and the two eyes were given fractionally different views of the same subject. I remember best Niagara Falls, incredibly three-dimensional, and interesting to me because I knew that Mother and Dad had started married life there.

Sometime that next winter Florrie had to leave us. She had "taken service" to help her sister and brother tide over the years while they waited for the apple orchard they had planted in the Okanagan Valley to reach maturity and start bearing apples. That time had come, and she was needed out west. We never forgot her. Every Christmas

she sent us a loving letter full of news of her brother and
sister and their life in Oyama, and a box of her own
home-made chocolates, and on my bedroom wall I had
her photograph in a silver frame. When I visited her
twenty years later on my first trip west, I got off the bus
looking for the tall woman I remembered, and there she
was, just like her photograph, but a little person who
came hardly above my shoulder.

In the fall of 1918 there was the Sunday of the false
alarm, when all the bells in Toronto rang for the end of
the war, and then we found out it was not yet true. But
the armistice came soon after, and I was taken uptown to
the front porch of a house on University Avenue just
north of Queen Street to see the victory parade, with
broad ranks of men in khaki marching down the wide
street, and everyone on the sidewalk waving flags and
shouting and crying.

Any prolonged jubilation about the end of the war
changed quickly to anxiety when the flu epidemic hit the
world in the autumn of 1918. It caused more deaths than
the war had, and was more unpredictable. People avoided
being in crowds and took all the precautions they could
think of, but still the streets seemed to be full of funerals.
When I went with Dad on his Sunday-afternoon long
walk we crossed to the south side of Kingston Road to
stay farther from the cemetery at St. John's Norway.
Even the air was suspect.

The incident that underlined for me the return of peace
happened on the Sunday morning that I went into the
kitchen, where Mother was getting dinner. There was a
pot on the stove, tightly covered.

"Can you keep a secret?" Mother asked, and she lifted the lid just enough to let me see and smell that the pot was full of potatoes. *Potatoes!* Was it two years since we had had them? I can smell them still.

2

Marjorie-and-Doris

ONE SATURDAY IN AUGUST OF 1918 a new family moved into the big white house next door to us. We saw the furniture being unloaded and carried up the walk, and later there was a small boy running around, and two girls. But it was not until Sunday afternoon that I had a chance to speak to one of them. A Salvation Army band was playing at the corner of Pine Avenue and Balsam, in front of their house. A fair, pretty girl, who seemed to be about Doug's age, came out on the lawn and stood watching. I stationed myself a respectful distance away. Two "Sally Anns" in their trim navy uniforms and bonnets and three men with instruments were giving a rousing concert of hymns, lively enough to set toes tapping and tempt us to sing along. But some rowdy boys whom I had never seen before were across the road, jeering and yelling at them rudely. I seized my opportunity. "Aren't they awful?" I ventured. "They're terrible," she agreed, and she told me

her name was Eleanor Beer. While we were still exchang-
ing tentative introductions her younger sister joined us
rather shyly, and so I met Marjorie.

She was smaller than Eleanor, slight, with short mousy
hair cut with a straight bang, very different from the thick
blonde pigtail that hung down my broad back. Although
she was nine, a year older than I and taller, I was the
sturdier in build. Nobody ever called either of us pretty;
we liked each other at once. In the weeks before school
opened we became friends, comfortable together, pleased
to discover that we had read the same books, both in love
with Anne of Green Gables and both still with secret
loyalty to our outgrown dolls. We were each entering
Grade Six (then called Senior Third) but, alas, at different schools. Marjorie was enrolled at Balmy Beach
School just across the road from our homes, and I was
half a mile away at Williamson Road School, where I had
been since kindergarten.

This made weekends all the more precious and we
looked forward eagerly to Saturdays when we were allowed to share picnics on the side porch of the Beers'
house. Marjorie's bedroom window faced mine, and we
contrived a private wake-up signal to give us time together before breakfast. We had a string long enough to
stretch from window to window, and each of us tied an
end to her big toe. The first to waken after daylight gave
a tug. We went to the window to acknowledge the signal,
and the morning was ours.

My parents were pleased with the friendship.
Marjorie's father was a doctor who had been with the
army in England and France, and Mother admired doctors, especially those who had been in the war. Dr. Beer

was still in active service, but stationed in Toronto. He was called for every morning by a uniformed driver in an automobile. This was a matter of some pride, for motor cars were still so uncommon that whenever one came up Balsam Avenue everyone's head turned to watch. On rare occasions when he was needed uptown on a Saturday morning, he would take Marjorie and me in the back seat for the ride. The Beers found us to be good neighbours and encouraged our growing intimacy.

Marjorie's parents were literary in their interests, active members of the Dickens Fellowship. Mine were practical, Mother a born organizer, Dad a tool-user, able to make things and always working at something. (Sixty-five years later my books stand on the shelves Dad made for me for my bedroom on Balsam Avenue.) Both Marjorie and I were readers and together we haunted the Beaches Library and explored a wider and wider range of books and authors. But Mother and Dad were game. I smile when I recall the summer evenings in the garden swing when they took turns reading *The Old Curiosity Shop* aloud to Doug and me and each other in emulation of the Beers.

Marjorie and I discovered an entrance to the crawl-space under the veranda that ran on two sides of the Beer house, and we used to creep in there on our hands and knees and sit in the dark corner nearest my house, smoking dry oak leaves in acorn pipes, playing characters called Jake and Bill. It was from that refuge that we overheard our mothers agreeing that we would both benefit from ballet lessons and that we should be enrolled in a Saturday-morning session up at the Margaret Eaton School of Expression, famous for its classes in all forms of physical training. Our mirth at the idea of our trying to be ballet dancers was matched by our delight at the prospect of travelling to town together every week.

We went west on the Queen Street car and transferred to the Belt Line, a route that circled the inner city and would take us up to Bloor Street. The cars were enclosed, each with a coal stove down at one end to provide warmth in winter. The conductor sat on a high perch in the centre, collecting fares. The trip was endlessly interesting. From where we boarded the car at Maclean we were taken past the first pond on our right and the whole of Scarborough Beach Park on our left, then on towards our own Beaches Library and Kew Gardens, with the real skating rink that was better than the pond. Farther on was the race-track where you could sometimes see horses running, then the car barns full of empty streetcars opposite the landmark house with the wonderful garden where the Ashbridge family still lived. They had once owned all the land around that part of east Toronto, including Ashbridge's Bay. West of their house Queen Street became shabbier until we got to the big furniture store at the corner of Broadview. We crossed the railway tracks and the Don River on an iron bridge with high girders and jerked along the part of Queen Street that had no gardens or trees at all, just mean little shops and a few factories. The Belt Line ran up Sherbourne Street, past its fine old brick mansions and Allan Gardens, and on beyond the very house my family had lived in when we first came to Toronto. Our stop came soon after that.

The classes were held in an imposing imitation Greek temple on Sherbourne Street near Bloor, but we were ill equipped to serve in the sanctuary. Two dancers more

inept would be difficult to imagine. We tried hard, feet at
right angles as demonstrated, arms down at the side, then
out, forward, up. "Again, please . . . Smoothly, dear . . .
Don't jerk . . . Again, please . . . " But it was a lost cause.
We did not become the graceful little girls Mother and
Mrs. Beer had hoped for.

Summer brought separation, eased by letters. Marjorie
was taken out west by her grandmother to meet her
Brandon cousins. I spent July at a table Dad had set up
under the trees, making a book as a birthday present for
Mother, writing the story and painting the illustrations.
Story-writing seemed a natural thing to do for anyone so
much in love with reading, and drawing and painting the
illustrations seemed equally natural. I don't suppose I
thought that Mother would be particularly interested in
the tale of a princess and a giant, but I was confident that
she would be pleased I had made it for her.

By the end of August a new house had been built on
the corner of Spruce Hill Road and Queen Street, and
the Beer family moved one street east and down the hill
to the proper doctor's residence and office that had been
made ready for them. Marjorie and I met or parted at the
corner of Sycamore and Spruce Hill, the half-way point.
"See you at Syc" was the word.

Balmy Beach School went no higher than Grade Six,
so in September Marjorie transferred to Williamson
Road and we were together, same room, same teacher,
and only two seats apart. It was probably on our walks
to and from school, arm in arm, that we fell into the habit
of being always on the same side, Marjorie on my right.
The time came when we were uncomfortable and
switched if we started out on the wrong side. This way

we fitted. But our friendship was not exclusive. We took two other girls into our fellowship to form the Quartette Club, with Marjorie as president and Doris as secretary. I think we were suffering from leadership ability and needed somebody to lead. I have forgotten the purpose of the club. We did have formal meetings and learned the rules of procedure, and we did hold a street fair on Queen Street to raise money for the Toronto Star Fresh Air Fund. We took the five or six dollars we earned up to the Home for Incurable Children and were taken through the hospital. I am still haunted by the image of those tots with heads enlarged to monstrous size.

In March, Dad and Mother were called into conference with the school principal and my teacher. Doris was "idling, not being sufficiently challenged." It was recommended that I be advanced to Senior Fourth, the high school entrance class. Once again we were separated during school hours, but together so happily at all other times that Marjorie-and-Doris became almost one word to our schoolmates. We were both instinctive actors and loved to tease, and that spring we thought it would be a great joke on everyone to pretend that we had had a fight and were not speaking to each other. Such tiffs were commonplace in our age group, but we knew that one between us would be an astonishment and an embarrassment to our circle. We talked it over, giggling, imagining what we would say, how we should act – and then knew we would do no such thing. Our friendship was sacred and we could not desecrate it.

Wonderful that two children who were so different
could grow to be so close. Marjorie was almost delicate,
apt to show fatigue by a bilious attack that would put her
to bed to recover her poise. Doris was stalky and strong,
with her mother's emotional energy, and the confidence to
take the lead in physical skills. Doris was a good student,
intellectual in her approach, with high marks in everything. Marjorie was top student in the humanities but had
no head for mathematics; her genius was with people. She
was always the president, the head of the committee, the
first to initiate a class project. She met everyone with a
warmth and interest that took her right through their
reserve and into their hearts. Marjorie was a poet with a
magical imagination and a delicious sense of fun.

My advance to high school at Malvern Collegiate was
momentous in some ways but it hardly rippled the surface
of our life together. There was no one there who could
offer me what Marjorie and I shared. We both intended
to become great authors, and each of us had in the works
several short stories and at least one full-length novel.
Two weeks after I had won the junior oratorical contest
at Malvern, Marjorie won the senior oratorical at Williamson Road. We published regularly (for each other) a
newspaper called "Passé Don Veul," a name without
meaning but with a sophisticated French ring to our ears.

In discussing our literary ambitions, we agreed, probably on her suggestion, to ask to be given diaries for
Christmas, so that we would be practising writing and
Improving Our Style. On New Year's Day 1922 each of
us began to keep a journal. Hers allowed one page a day,
mine was blank, which may be why I often wrote at great
length. My entry for January 3 reports the arrival of the

dressmaker, who came into residence to sew for anyone in the family who needed it, "so I had to be fitted and it was not till after two o'clock that I met Marjorie for the first time since the Friday night I slept over with her and went skating. My skates worked fine." In spite of the syntax I gather that we went skating on the day of the writing. My journal goes on to describe in detail the plot of the story that Marjorie had just completed and outlined to me. "While we talked and skated we promised each other that we would dedicate our first successful attempts to each other. I told Marjorie about Orphan Gracie and Fluff [short stories I had written], and she told me about her Vanity of Peggy [a long short story]. At last it was time for us to go home and we did, each greatly encouraged by the other's enthusiasm."

A few weeks later we wrote a verse play together, a one-act drama about a fairy kingdom suffering under persecution from mischievous elves. I suspect that its plot owed much to *Lamb's Tales from Shakespeare*. It contained some slight variety of character, a modicum of conflict, and a happy ending. Our elders were impressed, and, thanks no doubt to Mother's influence, it was produced as part of a concert put on in the basement of St. Aidan's Church to raise money for the building of the Memorial Hall. There were musical numbers, dances, and recitations, but to Marjorie and me these were merely preparation for the triumphant climax provided by the play. As the curtain closed at the end of it, there were cries of "Author, author!" The rector, Dr. Cotton, already a genial friend, called us up to the stage to be presented with flowers. My diary's detailed description of the event concludes with the declaration, "This day is an epoch in my life."

Our diaries were not for sharing even with each other. They were for making our own discoveries of who we were, and learning to find words for our most secret thoughts. Having found the right words, however, it is very likely that we then shared the thoughts. We could be sure of the other's understanding.

Art at that time was far more mysterious and distant to me than writing. I drew constantly during class, keeping a blank exercise book handy for the purpose, and careful that, whatever my hands were doing, my ear was on the alert. The teachers learned that I was still paying attention and didn't bother me. But I drew for my own amusement and didn't think of my scribbles as art. Drawing and painting came naturally to me, but there were two other girls at school who could draw ladies better than I could, which kept me modest about my ability. Although I chose the art option at high school, nothing at Malvern nourished my talent or my interest. We were taught a recipe for making backgrounds in water-colour and spent some useless hours trying to copy the shape of a detached nose in clay. On the other hand the courses in English and the teachers were inspiring, and my marks in literature and composition were high. Writing seemed a possible career, and university a route that could lead me in that direction. Marjorie was already writing and being published in the "Young Canada" page of the *Globe*. She and I were confident that we would be Canada's next L.M. Montgomerys, and we used to amuse ourselves by playing at being "future us" and writing notes back and forth describing conferences with our publishers about our latest bestsellers.

3

Silver Island

EDEN TO ME is a ten-acre island in Muskoka with a cottage that we rented for the first time in the summer of 1922. Mr. Ferrier, who owned the island and spent his summers in the other cottage there, was understood to be very particular about whom he rented it to, and came all the way from Mimico on the other side of Toronto to look us over. Mr. Ferrier was superintendent of the Mimico Industrial School (for "bad boys"), a formidable person. Doug and I were instructed to call him "Sir." It is the only time in my whole childhood that I can recall being briefed about company manners.

We were careful to be very polite to the tall broad stranger. After some exchange of pleasantries and general information that must have been reassuring, he brought out a map that showed the island in Lake Muskoka, about half-way between Bala and Port Carling, and a snapshot of a small cottage almost hidden by trees. And he told

Mother and Dad about the safe sandy beach and the good drinking water that you pulled up from the well by lowering a bucket on a rope. He explained that a supply boat called once a week to sell fresh fruit and vegetables, and that we could buy milk from the farmer who lived on the mainland on the way to Mortimer's Point, where we would have to go for the mail. Eddie Mortimer owned the cows, and also the launch that could be hired to bring us from the train station at Bala Park. A rowboat was supplied with the cottage, and Mortimer's Point was about a mile and a half up the lake. We were accepted!

Best of all was that Marjorie was coming too. Dr. Beer wanted to take Mrs. Beer to England and show her the places he had been to in the war, and Mother had agreed to have Marjorie as a second daughter for the whole summer. We could hardly believe in such good fortune. The two mothers employed Mrs. Bennett, the enormously stout dressmaker who lived down on Spruce Hill Road, to make us "play-suits." These consisted of knee-length black sateen bloomers and short black sateen tunics as shapeless as the two little girls wearing them. They had square necklines bordered with a two-inch band of coloured cretonne, pink for Marjorie, blue for me. No bride looks at her trousseau with more pride than we felt in these creations.

Ken, after his second year at university, was at work as a deckhand on SS *Cayuga*, one of the passenger steamers on the run across Lake Ontario to Queenston. Doug and I were writing exams while Mother made lists and packed. When the great day came, Dr. Beer drove Mother and Marjorie and me to the Don Station down below the Queen Street bridge. Dad and Doug had gone with the canoe and the trunk in Mr. Oliphant's hired truck and were already there on the platform, standing guard over the luggage.

My most vivid memory of the trip itself is of green plush upholstery in the coach and the smell of dust and coal smoke mingled with the pungency of the sardine sandwiches and oranges that Mother had packed for our lunch. Dad got off the train at every stop and walked along the platform to the baggage car to be sure that the canoe was still safe.

When we arrived at Bala Park, Doug helped Dad carry the canoe down to the boat dock, and we found there, among the luggage and freight piled up along the edge, ten big cartons addressed to "George McCarthy, c/o Eddie Mortimer, Bala Park." Our summer's supply of groceries had arrived from Eaton's. Now, if only Eddie Mortimer would come too! It was hot. We were tired and sticky after the long train trip. And there was no sign of anyone looking for us. But the wait was not without drama. There was a lady (dare I call her that?) sitting on one of the posts on the dock, and she was *smoking*. I was too embarrassed to stare, but there was no doubt about it. I had never before seen such a thing.

An open launch rounded the point and came towards us, with a tall lean man in the front, tanned and wind-blown. Dad had taught me to paddle, and I was used to a canoe and a rowboat, but this was my first time in a motor boat. We watched Eddie start the engine with a crank, just like a car, and suddenly we were moving, faster and faster. Marjorie and I sat side by side squeezing each other's hand, speechless with excitement.

Half an hour later we could see ahead of us distant

shapes of islands. "That's her!" shouted Eddie above the noise of the water and the engine. He was pointing to the largest island, the one with a single tall pine tree towering above the wooded shoreline. As we came closer we saw a dock, bright against the dark trees, and an arc of white sand curving away from it. Soon we could recognize the low, wide house behind the birches, and as the launch drew alongside the dock, there was Mr. Ferrier coming down a path to meet us. A skinny boy followed him and began carrying bags and boxes up the path before we had even finished unloading them. He disappeared with the luggage up the left fork in the path, but we were taken to the right to the Ferrier cottage to "meet Mama."

Mama was enthroned in a big wicker armchair on the porch, with two grown-up daughters in attendance. Her legs were "bad," and it was soon clear that everyone was kept running to save them. Amy was the elder daughter who stayed home and kept house. We thought "old maid" when we met her. Irene, who taught school, looked livelier and showed some interest in Doug as a tennis partner. He was a good-looking, well-grown teen-ager by this time, worth some interest.

Marjorie and I were cautiously silent until the courtesies had been concluded and we were escorted by Irene to our own cottage. Eric, the boy from the notorious school, had already piled all our bags and boxes on the porch and brought us a pail of fresh water from the well. We had arrived.

It was a wooden cottage, painted brown with white trim, unlined inside, but decorated between the two-by-fours with cut-outs from magazines that Marjorie and I gleefully reorganized and supplemented during the summer. The living room had a veranda across the front and a bedroom on either side. The one on the right was larger and was promptly labelled "the harem" because Mother and I were to share the big bed in it, and Marjorie was to use the cot. Dad and Doug made do with the little room on the other side. Behind the living room was the kitchen with a woodstove, and off that a back porch big enough for the table that soon became the focus of our cottage life. When we were not around it, we were on the veranda or in the lake.

Or exploring the island. A path through dense undergrowth up a hill at the back led to the "little house," a two-holer, much to Marjorie's and my delight. A second path ran through more open woods with boulders half covered with pine needles and led to the big pine that we had seen from the launch. We named it "Spyglass" and buried at its foot a bottle in which we hid a letter to be opened by the finder in 1937, fifteen years thence, an unimaginably distant future.

The trail to the tennis court that Irene had cleared in the centre of the island was lined with fragrant hemlock undergrowth. Beyond the tennis court the trail continued to the other side of the island, and to a third cottage. We came to realize that Mr. Ferrier regretted ever having sold even one lot, but Marjorie and I found the widow who lived there with her teen-age son very cordial. She invited the whole family over one evening to hear our very first "tube" radio. It had a loudspeaker, and we could all listen to it without earphones.

To our eyes the view from the front veranda of the cottage was perfection. Through a light screen of birch and pine trees we looked across a quarter of a mile of lake

to Dunbarton, a beautiful little island with a picturesque
log cottage set on a rock against a background of pines.
I was glad that I had brought my school paintbox and
knew that I must try to paint the scene. Other small
islands lay between it and the far shore. Hidden by the
woods behind the Ferrier cottage was a bay with a dock
much larger than the one in front. The water was deep
there, and Mother soon discovered that it was the best
place to fish. She would sit on the end of the dock for
many a blissful hour, wrapped in her old ankle-length
sweater, catching bass. Marjorie and I were privileged to
clean them on the rock beside the dock, throwing the
scraps to the gulls.

It was in this back bay that the supply boat docked.
When we heard its horn we ran. It was not as large as the
passenger boats, the *Sagamo* and the *Ahmic*, but it was as
big inside as a shop, and we carried baskets of vegetables
and fruit back to the cottage after each visit. We had a
cooler, a room that had been built into the side of the slope
below the cottage. It was as cold as any cave and kept
things fresh without ice. Milk we stored in the shade on
the front porch, in a granite milk tin set in a pan of water,
and wrapped in a cloth that acted like a wick and stayed
moist enough for the wind to keep the milk chilled. We
shared the chores. Doug carried the water and the firewood. Marjorie and I did the washing-up.

That was the summer we learned to dive, spending
hours in and out of the lake, groping along the sandy
bottom after the metal ring we used as a lure, dumping
the canoe and climbing back into it. We felt like fish.
Eventually we could swim right across to Dunbarton
with the rowboat as escort. At the beginning of the

summer we rowed for the milk and the mail, but by
August, if the evening was calm, we were allowed to go
by canoe. We came home as the sun was low, paddling
towards the great early star in the south-west that I still
think of as "Goldie."

Doug's friend Laurie Bullen was up for a few weeks.
The two boys, emboldened by mutual support, began
paying court to Miss Harriman, a pretty American university student who was a guest at Dunbarton. They
would hang around Dunbarton and take her out in the
canoe, and they began to wear enormous wooden keys
that they had carved to tease her about being a member
of the Kappa Kappa Gamma sorority.

An event of every summer was the annual regatta
organized by the Kettles Summer Resident Association.
The Kettles, a small cluster of rocks that broke the surface
of the water about half-way from Silver Island to
Mortimer's Point, were so named because of the way the
water boiled around them even when the lake was comparatively calm. There were twenty or more cottages in
the area and four or five children or young people in each.
A cottage with a big dock and diving board, or even a
diving tower, would be offered as a place to hold the
regatta, and when the day came it would be the goal of
all the canoes, rowboats, dinghies, and launches in the
district. There were contests for every age, in every skill.
Marjorie and Doug and I entered everything for which
we were eligible, cheered on by Mother watching from
the shore. I have long since forgotten if we won anything,
but I have never forgotten my paralysis of horror when,
changing out of a wet bathing suit in the boat-house, I
was surprised by the entrance of a boy!

All summer long at Silver Island there were family games, cribbage, all the pencil games we knew, and hearts, that poor relation of bridge. Mother once offered a chocolate bar as a prize for the winner, but quickly withdrew the offer as she wondered if it might teach us to gamble. We laughed at her then. We laughed at one another, the cottage rocked with laughter. There were evenings when Mother feared that our hilarity might be disturbing the Ferriers.

Marjorie and I were used to slipping into many character roles with each other. One of us would assume a voice, and the other would pick up the cue. Sometimes we were Bill and Jake, ruffians who lived in the mountains. Often she was Teddy – Edward, Prince of Wales – and I was a lady of the court. We were avid collectors of photographs and clippings about royalty. We played our future selves, the famous authors, and we read together. Marjorie had been given *Anne's House of Dreams* for her birthday, and we read *David Copperfield* that summer, not aloud, but keeping up with each other so that we could discuss each incident and character.

Silver Island was in a Methodist enclave. There were famous Methodist names up and down the mainland near us: Endicott, Moore, Rogers. But since there was only one little church in the whole district and it was Anglican, every Sunday evening one of the cottages became the gathering point for a song service. Families came in all manner of craft, dressed almost as if for church. Most of them left their boats at the dock and carried cushions up to the veranda, but some young people stayed on the water, adding what Marjorie and I considered a romantic dimension to the scene. There were hymn-books enough for everyone. Irene Ferrier played an autoharp when there was no piano or parlour pump-organ. Mother loved it, and her golden voice poured like honey over the water. As we left for home in the deepening dark, the lake was dotted with lights from the small craft going their separate ways, and Mother was still humming, "Now God be with you till we meet again."

Before we left at the end of August Dad had arranged to rent the cottage for the next year, but the following spring we began to fear that we might not be able to go. Our hopes for a second summer at Silver Island hung on Ken's academic results. He had come home from his university exams in despair, and if he had to write a "supplemental" in the fall there would be no cottage for us. Mother was grimly resolved to stay at home to keep house for him. On Friday, June 1, 1923, I wrote in my diary: "I was sitting on the veranda and I heard Mother on the phone say, 'Oh! that's the best news you could give me. Oh, we're so glad!' I just knew. I knew Ken's results were out and I knew Ken had passed. I ran upstairs and hugged all the comforters and thanked God. All our terrible despairing haunting fears that he would fail or have a sup and that we couldn't go to Silver Island were groundless. WE CAN GO."

Go we did, and Marjorie too. Her parents had been so delighted with the brown healthy girl that Mother had returned to them the previous August that she was part of our plan from the beginning. But the Beers plotted to surprise us this second summer and rented Dunbarton

for a month, sight unseen, without telling even Marjorie.
Fortunately they were delighted with it. The Beers and
the McCarthys shared meals at one island or the other.
Doug and Eleanor swam, played tennis and paddled
together, becoming good friends. Mrs. Beer's parents
came for a visit and Dr. Beer was there for several
weekends. It was a sociable July.

Dad was with us for his holidays in August and let us
teach him to dive. Much of his time on the island was
spent cutting dead trees and sawing and splitting them
into firewood. When he had a good woodpile stacked up
he went on to paint the cottage for Mr. Ferrier, and we
gave him an occasional hand with that job. Dad loved
work and was a meticulous craftsman. He had noticed
the condition of the cottage and was glad to be of help to
Mr. Ferrier. Both Mother and Dad prided themselves on
leaving any place better than they found it.

Seen from Silver Island, Dunbarton was a charming
composition of trees, cottage, and rock, set against distant
shore. I found it so satisfying and beautiful that I wanted
to capture it on paper. I had no theories of art and no
technique of water-colour, but I had an accurate eye and
some experience in mixing paints to get tones or hues
intermediate to the pure colours in the school paintbox.
I carefully copied what I saw, with results that are predictably pedestrian and muddy. Two of my paintings have
survived. It is interesting to me now to see that I did
observe the gradation of tone in the sky from the horizon
up to the zenith, and that I invented a convention to
describe the stonework on which the cottage stood.

We had four summers there before Dad found a cottage to buy, in a different part of Muskoka. During the

third summer Mother was struggling with ill health. She
sent up Marjorie and me with Doug and his friend Harvey Graham, chaperoned by our beloved Eleanor Baskerville. "Aunt Nell" was a tiny hunchbacked woman
who had been Marjorie's home-room teacher in her last
year at public school. She had given music lessons to both
Doug and me, and she had given me a much more
precious gift, a bird guide and a book of wild flowers. I
was at the right age to be a collector, and thanks to her I
began to "collect" birds, keeping a list of those I had
identified and where seen, as well as all the wild flowers
I found. She was full of fun and gave us a merry fortnight
before Mother came up to take over.

The last summer at Silver Island I had to be content
with someone else as my special companion. Marjorie
was out west, experiencing for the first time the joys of a
girls' camp. Life changed. There were new worlds.

4

Two Steps

ONE SUNDAY AFTERNOON in June 1921, just before I turned eleven, Dad invited me to come with him for a paddle on Lake Ontario, and to pack a supper so that we could go a bit farther than if we had to be home for tea. I leapt at the chance: the first time I had had the responsibility of being his bow paddler and the full privilege of his companionship. The canoe was kept at the Beach, in a boat-house at the foot of Fernwood Park Avenue, but we had to carry the paddles and cushions from home as well as the basket that Mother had packed for our picnic. I was proud to have my share of the load, and to be able to lift my end of the canoe down from the rack and help to carry it across to the water's edge for launching.

There was very little wind, hardly enough for the one or two sailboats that were out in the lake beyond us. We paddled east, with the sun behind us, past the Balmy

Beach Canoe Club, past the old Mann estate in the
Fallingbrook area, which was still all wooded, and past
the Hunt Club, which had for the McCarthys such glam-
orous memories.

The Toronto Hunt Club is still impressive, a fine stone
mansion set with its own golf course on the edge of the
lake above a high sand and clay bluff, although the fox
hunting, with its dogs and kennels, moved up to north
Toronto many years ago. The section of the golf course
north of Kingston Road has been subdivided and built
over. During its heyday, after the war, Dad and Mother
and Kenneth used to be invited to a big family Christmas
dinner there every year. Grandma Moffatt's cousin was
married to Captain Trowell, who was the secretary and
had the privilege of using the clubhouse and staff for his
own Christmas party. For the two years before Captain
Trowell retired, Doug and I were considered old enough
to be included. There was a baronial dining room, a table
to seat thirty, silver shining, glassware sparkling, a huge
fire blazing on a hearth at one end of the room. For me,
the most exciting features were the row of waiters in
uniform standing behind us, and ginger ale as common as
milk. The first time I was invited, I drank the ginger ale
so eagerly that I had room for nothing else. The next year
saw me wiser, and I was able to last even to the marvel of
the Baked Alaska, an undreamed-of sophistication. Dad
danced with me after dinner, and so did Ken, and the
Trowells' big grown-up son, Harry, who was light on his
feet in spite of his size. There was a Paul Jones to mix
everyone up. The older ladies and gentlemen were in
another room playing cards. Afterwards, for the Mc-

Carthys, there was a long walk home in the snowy cold, upheld by the excitement of the whole wonderful Christmas that lay behind us.

Beyond the Hunt Club, the Scarborough bluffs became bare and sculptural, eroded into sharp peaks and cut with ravines. In those days there was no Bluffers Park, no marina, only the narrow strip of beach, and for an hour or so Dad and I paddled close to the shore, watching for birds. We came at last to the remains of the old lake freighter the *Alexandra*, which had foundered during the war in a violent autumn storm. Rumour had it that she was worn out and heavily insured. She had run aground and broken up, and her cargo of canned goods minus their labels had been washed up and strewn for most of a mile along the shore. Ken and some of his friends had ridden out on their bicycles, salvaged a few tins, and brought them home. Now all that was visible of the old ship was the round top of the boiler and part of a funnel. Gulls flew from it, screaming, as we approached. We circled it curiously, then decided to land on the beach nearby where a deep ravine came down to the shore.

We had our picnic there on the sand, building a small fire just for the fun of it. When the sun had dropped behind the top of the bluffs, and the air grew cooler, we packed up and took to the water again, far enough out from shore to feel the sun's warmth as we paddled home. It was the first time I had known my father as a friend.

At the end of that summer I entered high school at Malvern Collegiate, Toronto's newest secondary school, built two blocks north of Kingston Road and serving Scarborough students as well as those from the east end of Toronto. Doug was already there, in Grade Ten, and although Ken was now at the University of Toronto in pre-meds he was well remembered at Malvern. When he was in Third Form Mother had been out on the front lawn sweeping up leaves one afternoon when Mr. Graham, the chemistry teacher, came walking down the street on his way home.

He raised his hat to her. "Good afternoon, Mrs. Mc-Carthy. Lovely day. Would you like to know where your son is?"

"Kenneth? Well, where is he then?"

"He is in the chemistry lab, down on his hands and knees scrubbing the floor. I wish I could hang him from the ceiling and make him scrub that too."

"Whatever happened?" asked Mother.

Mr. Graham laughed. "He tried an independent experiment with some chemicals in his inkwell, and he's cleaning up the results of the explosion."

The blue splotch was still on the ceiling when Doug and I graduated from Malvern, but poor Mr. Graham was killed by an automobile as he was crossing the street towards the school the year that I was in Grade Eleven. He was my home-form master, and it was my first personal contact with death. He was old (probably in his fifties), with silvery hair, but we had respected and liked him and we were all shocked. It was his wife who had directed our play at St. Aidan's, and his son Harvey was Doug's friend who had been up with us at Silver Island. Mother moved down into the Graham house to help Mrs. Graham through the days before the funeral. It was still the custom to set up the open casket in the living room, marking the front door with a wreath hung with purple or black ribbon, and to receive friends and neighbours at home. On one of those days Mother asked me to bring something down to her. I have forgotten what it was, but I have never forgotten my cold fear when she asked me if I would like to come in and "see Mr. Graham." I couldn't speak. I shook my head and turned back up the hill, blinded with tears, not of grief but of terror at the thought of looking at a dead person.

Less dreadful than death to me, but more mysterious, was birth. Mother had prepared me for menstruation by a little talk one day when I was home from school and in bed with a cold. She explained that, when a woman was married, God planted a seed in her, which grew to be a baby, and that the womb had to be kept ready for this great event by a monthly housecleaning. She provided me with a supply of linen napkins and introduced me to the monthly horror of wearing them pinned back and front to a belt, like a loincloth, keeping their existence a dark secret from the men and the boys, and looking after their laundering myself. No wonder menstruation was referred to, in girls' talk, as "the curse," and mentioned only to excuse a sick headache or bilious attack and never in mixed company.

After the summer the Beers had spent at Dunbarton across from Silver Island, Marjorie was allowed to tell me the secret she had nursed since June, that Mrs. Beer was going to have another baby. Marjorie was thrilled. When I talked to Mother about it, she said she thought it was "disgusting." "But Mother," I protested, "you said you couldn't help it if you were married." "You can help it if you want to," said Mother stiffly.

Marjorie and I spent many hours that autumn wondering aloud to each other how it all happened, and how the baby got out. Eventually her father put into her hands *Men, Women and God*, a book that told us the facts at long last, explaining sex and marriage and babies in the context of human love, and convincing us that life was even more wonderful and beautiful than we could have imagined. Poor Mother. It is a great pity that she didn't have such a book when she was young. Poor Dad too. It must have been rough being married to a beautiful, spirited girl with twisted, Victorian ideas about sex.

Ken and Betty Caswell were "going steady." The Caswells lived only a few doors south of us on Balsam Avenue. Edward Caswell was a publisher, the editor of *Canadian Singers and Their Songs*, an anthology of poetry that reproduced each poem in the poet's own handwriting. Marjorie had impressed me with how wonderful it was to know someone linked so closely to the great. There were three girls in the Caswell family. Betty, the eldest, lovely and serene, was Kenneth's girl all through high school, and he still dated her after he went to university, although he was a bit of a flirt and played the field then. We all loved Betty and found her easier to know than Ken. But we didn't betray him on the day when she came with us across to Niagara on the *Cayuga*. Ken was a deck steward and had one of his other dates on board that day. With some fancy footwork he managed to keep the two girls on different decks and perform his duties too.

Betty, who was on the staff of the Beaches Library,

gave me my first paid job, a session after school sorting
books and replacing them on shelves, rewarded with an
envelope containing my wages, twenty-five cents. I kept
that coin for a long time. It was too precious to spend.
Much the same feeling must have moved Dad to ask for
his first professional pay in gold, and then to have it made
into Mother's wedding ring.

Betty's sister Evelyn was a senior at Malvern when I
entered, and Marjorie and I came to know her when she
directed us in a play based on Dickens's *A Christmas Carol*.
She and I became friends, bonded by our common appreciation of the "Elsie" books. I had inherited the whole set,
twenty-eight novels about the pious child whose story
inspired my mother's generation with religious fervour.
At eight and nine I read them with serious respect, but
by fourteen I found them hilarious. Ev and I used to have
"evenings with Elsie," reading excerpts and collapsing in
mirth. Mother pretended to be shocked at us, but she was
not convincing.

The third Caswell sister, Shirley, was younger, and had
different interests. It was much later that she became
important to us all.

At Malvern too the young people were forming couples. Doug and Eleanor were ahead of Marjorie and me
and part of a group of classmates who gave grown-up
parties to which we, as younger sisters, were sometimes
invited. This group became very good friends and by the
time they were in Fourth Form they had begun choosing
partners. When the school dances were held they were
already in couples. Not so with Marjorie and me. In our
crowd there was tremendous ferment for weeks in advance, with speculation as to who would invite whom,

and much secret anxiety. No self-respecting girl made the advances, at least according to Mother. If an invitation were proffered, awkwardly during some chance encounter as the classes passed in the hall between periods, or during the brief lunch break, the level of anxiety stepped up sharply. What to wear? How to dance without falling all over his feet? What to talk about?

The conventions demanded that the boy call for his girl and walk her to the dance. Once there, he was responsible for filling her programme. These programmes were folders decorated with ribbons of red and black, the Malvern colours, and printed inside with twenty numbered lines, one labelled "supper dance." The lad who took you put his name in the first, last, and supper dance slots, and while you were greeting the other girls in the classroom set up as a ladies' dressing room, powdering your nose yet again, putting in time, he did his best to find seventeen friends willing to dance with you. Of course the boys traded. "You give me one and I'll take one of yours." If my gawky escort returned to me before the first dance with many blanks on the programme, I wanted to die. Instead, I kept the bright smile on my face and, with body as tense as my emotions, held out my arms to receive him. We danced with my left hand on his shoulder, his right around my back to guide me, and our other hands clasped and held stiffly out to the side. "I'm sorry," as one of us stepped on the other's foot. "Oh, that was my fault." I suppose we did sometimes have other things to say to each other.

I made a tremendous investment in a school dance. My hair would be professionally waved and curled for the occasion, and I would be in my very best sleeveless silk dress, belted fashionably around the hips, bust as flat as binding could make it. By the time I was in Third Form, and being invited, the short skirts of the early Twenties were lengthening. At least I was spared the former agony of wondering if the tops of my stockings and my garters were showing at the back when I raised my arms. There was a brief-lived fashion that year of wearing a bright little silk handkerchief held by a ribbon tied around the ankle.

What a relief when my partner was Laurie Bullen. He was as familiar as a brother, and teased and laughed with me while we danced. Giggling at his sallies eased my tension for the moment. Supper came as a welcome break, bringing other girls and their partners to share the talk. I envied Beth Mader, whose hair was naturally curly and whose poise seemed equally natural. The misery of not being invited to the dance was equalled only by the misery of trying to live up to its demands.

The walk home was better because it was apt to be in groups of couples whose ways lay together. There was no thought of good-night kisses or of inviting him in to prolong the ordeal. We had both "had a lot of fun, thanks very much." Sometimes Mother had been there as a chaperone among the row of adults parked on chairs along the edge of the dance floor. When I came in, she was predictably critical of the music, of the way the boys danced these days, and of my hair. School dances are among the few nightmares of my youth.

Outdoor parties were better. Marjorie and I were included in some memorable winter hikes, long sunny days spent skiing, snowshoeing, tobogganing on the hills along the creek valley of Taylor's Bush. Lunch was made over a fire, with bacon hanging from a sharp stick spitting into the flame and eaten rubbery or charred, in cold bread. There was a tinned camp coffee syrup, stirred sweet and strong into hot water, very good. Pairing was not essential until after we had straggled back to somebody's home and shed our wet wools in the front hall, and were dancing to a gramophone record. Then you might be offered an escort home. If not, it didn't matter. I had no fear of the dark or of walking alone anywhere at the Beach.

Dad had conditioned me to feel that nature and the out-of-doors were an important part of my heritage. He was one of the early conservationists who had formed an organization, called Men of the Trees, dedicated to planting rather than cutting. The McCarthys never had a Christmas tree, taught by him to prefer a row of stockings hanging from the mantelpiece. He took me one night to hear the great Jack Miner and see slides of the bird sanctuary for Canada geese that he had established at his home near Kingsville.

More surprising, in retrospect, was the night that Dad invited me at the last minute to the Royal Alexandra to see Walter Hampden in *Hamlet*. Hampden was a big name in theatre in the Twenties. We were given the last two seats in the house at the end of the last row in the gods. What a performance! The audience was spellbound, and I felt that I had discovered a new side of my father.

The summer I turned sixteen was the first time we went to our own cottage in Muskoka. Sometime during the winter Dad had bought an old one-storey farmhouse overlooking a bay on Lake Muskoka, accessible by boat from Beaumaris, which in turn was accessible by steamer from Gravenhurst. Our arrival at the cottage was traumatic. There was no dock; we and our luggage and supplies were landed on the small sand beach from a launch that had only its nose on the shore and was rocking with every wavelet. Mother climbed up the slope to the house, looked through the cottage, and announced, "I'm not staying here, George." Poor Dad! He knew that it needed a lot of work, but he could visualize the delightful haven it eventually became and so could I. Mother could see only the newspapers pasted over the cracks in the walls and the shabby paint on the floor. Fortunately there was no way she could leave, and by the time the new cots and mattresses were out of their crates and the beds made up, the food unpacked, and the first meal under way, she began to notice the big bay window in the kitchen with its view down through trees to the lake she had learned to love so well at Silver Island. She had also discovered that the cookstove was a good one, and she was soon beguiled by the smell of wood smoke.

Before doing the cosmetic work inside the old house, Dad and I reshingled the roof. We rowed the three miles across Lake Muskoka to the sawmill at Milford Bay, loaded the whole supply of cedar shingles into the rowboat until there was hardly an inch of freeboard at the gunwale, and so home, Dad at the oars, Doris high in the stern, paddling and keeping the boat straight. It was much later that we learned we had been a sensation to the boys at the mill. I think they expected to see us capsized, swimming about and clinging to a bundle of shingles. The

fortnight spent on the roof working with Dad is one of
the best memories of my teens. He was a good craftsman,
knowing all the professional ways of making the roof
weathertight and keeping the rows uniform and true. We
were up on the steep side of the roof by nine in the
morning. Mother would come out into the sunshine and
hang up a washing with a word of praise for our progress
and some consultation about lunch. She was able to buy
fresh stewing lamb from the local farmer and throw in
with it onions, carrots, potatoes, whatever, until she had
a fine big potful, which she hoped would last for a couple
of days. Dad and I would descend, ravenous, and polish
it off.

By four in the afternoon I was tired of work and
climbed down for a swim and a leisurely removal of
slivers from my poor legs and seat. How those shingles
splintered! Dad hammered steadily on until he was called
for supper, and sometimes he put in another hour or two
before dark. I used to marvel at his will to stay with it. I
have learned since then the pull of a job like that.

We promised ourselves a holiday together when we
had finished making the cottage habitable, a week's canoe
trip with a tent somewhere, perhaps down the Moon
River to Georgian Bay. I think it is the only promise that
Dad ever broke.

5

The Bliss of Growth

EVEN NOW, sixty years later, I am not sure how objec-
tively I can look back on my teens. Rapture was commonplace, and although I seldom experience the same
intensity of joy now, nothing in my life since then denies
the reality of the emotions of those days, or the truth of
the insights I was led to. My horizons were enlarging and
I was responding to the ideals presented to me at church
and at school.

We sincerely believed that the 1914-1918 horror had
been a war to end war, and that the League of Nations
was the new way for the world to settle all disputes. Just
as the nineteenth century had presumably abolished slav-
ery forever, so the twentieth had ended war. Mother's
generation had achieved the vote for women, so that
universal suffrage was taken for granted. Canada was a
peaceful country where men, women, and even children
could walk safely day and night. Dad and Mother talked

a lot about the high cost of living, and we were taught to be careful with money and food, but poverty meant leaving school before graduation to go to a job, not hunger. Dad believed in public ownership of important utilities like hydro and the railway and always travelled Canadian National, but he considered himself a Conservative and could listen dispassionately to both sides of a political discussion. I grew up during Prohibition; alcohol was unknown to me; bootlegging was a word only. I remember Mother in tears in the kitchen one day because she had discovered Ken smoking a cigarette. The Twenties in my experience were not roaring, whatever their subsequent reputation, and the loving atmosphere of the home of my childhood was normal among my neighbours and school friends. Evil I knew as thoughtlessness, selfishness, complacency, and laziness. I prayed sincerely to be delivered from them.

In 1925, while Marjorie was out west with her grandparents for the summer, they arranged for her to spend a few weeks in a girls' camp in the Okanagan Valley. She came back with stars in her eyes and a vision of girls around the world joining hands in a fellowship of unity and understanding. She was in love with Mary Allison, the leader who had shown her this dream, and with the teen-agers who had shared it with her. She became part of the Canadian Girls in Training movement.

CGIT was an interdenominational Canada-wide experiment in religious education, sponsored by the major Protestant churches. Teen-aged girls were organized into groups, twelve or fewer in each, with an adult to lead them in Bible study on Sunday and in a midweek program of projects that were "purposed, planned, carried out, and

evaluated" by the girls themselves. It was hoped that by
studying, working, and playing together in this way they
could discover what Christianity really was and learn to
live it. Mary Allison, who had directed Marjorie's western
camp, was the national secretary, coordinating the program across Canada, and maintaining liaison with the
YWCA, the Girl Guides, and other youth organizations.
Jessie Macpherson did the same work for Ontario.

Marjorie's home church was Beech Avenue Methodist
Church, and she became deeply involved in its CGIT
group. Her leader was Louise Boothe, a librarian at the
Beaches Library, the young woman who pioneered the
concept of making a neighbourhood library into a focus
of community activity in music, drama, and art. I was
admitted to the edge of the group, getting to know the
other girls and Louise, painting scenery for the Christmas
play they were producing. Marjorie was soon on the
council that linked all the Toronto groups, making new
friends among the girls and the leaders she met there, and
full of plans to go to an Ontario CGIT camp the following
summer.

"March 27, 1926: Saw M a wee today. Mother says if
I get enough money from the sale of my bike I can go to
CGIT camp. I wonder if M would resent my going there
at all. I shall try to find out. I don't think she would but I
certainly don't want to go unless she wants me as much
as I want to go." Marjorie promptly laughed my misgivings away and convinced me that I was welcome in every
area of her life.

Jealousy, which I recognized as a sin, was probably
my greatest temptation. Marjorie's world was expanding
daily, bringing her close to national and provincial lead-

ers, young women of god-like glamour to us all. Marjorie loved them at sight and was able to express her love with such spontaneous simplicity that they in turn welcomed her into their personal lives as well as into their work. There were times when I felt that she had left me far behind. We both complained that we never saw each other. To give us needed time together we planned an adventure after camp, a week in the country, reading, walking, catching up. Aunt Nell Baskerville found us a farmhouse to stay at, and the arrangements were all made. But first – camp!

Normandale, on a cliff above Lake Erie not far from Port Dover, was a big field rising to a long hill that held the wooden dining pavilion, known as the "shack." Farther along the hillside was Round Top, the treed knoll where we sat on the grass for worship services and study groups. On the other side of the dining hall was a tall flagpole, with space around it for all sixty of us to stand in a circle for the morning ceremonial flag-raising and the recitation of the "Salutation to the Dawn."

> Look to this day
> For it is life, the very life of life.
> In its brief course
> Lie all the verities and realities of your existence.
> The bliss of growth,
> The glory of action,
> The splendour of beauty.
> For yesterday is but a dream
> and tomorrow is only a vision,
> But today well lived
> Makes every yesterday a dream of happiness

And every tomorrow a vision of hope.
Look well therefore to this day
Such is the salutation to the dawn.

From the hillside we looked down to the L-shaped arrangement of twenty white tents bright in the morning sun. The sun seemed to shine more brilliantly at Normandale than anywhere else in the world. We separated after flag-raising and each of us went alone to some special spot she had chosen for Morning Watch, the twenty minutes of solitude with a little book that was to help us find ways to think about God and give thanks for the love and beauty surrounding us. I found myself a nest in long grass on the very edge of the cliff, where I could watch the waves making patterns as they followed one another in to the edge of foam along the shore. I felt breathless with the beauty of the world and the joy of being at Normandale with Marjorie and with Jessie Macpherson as Big Chief.

We sang through breakfast and every other meal, gaining daily more confidence and unity. Tent-tidying came next, not the high point of the day for Marjorie and me although a time for much hilarity. Our tent-mates were congenial and co-operative, but none of us cared enough to spend time on the flower arrangements and such refinements that won for other tents the best-of-the-day flag. After morning worship on Round Top came Bible study in small groups with a leader, then a break that was often used for more informal discussion. Late in the morning all met together again for Council Hour, a time for camp business, special guests, learning a new song, whatever. After rest hour in the afternoon there were optional interest groups such as camp craft, handi-crafts, or nature study. I chose something that I hoped was sex education, but the dear Camp Mother who led it was of no use to me. She advised us never to "do anything that we wouldn't want our husbands to know." I still didn't know what you *could* do!

Evenings were for campfires, stories, games, and skits, ending when we stood in a circle, arms around one another, and sang taps.

> Day is done,
> Gone the sun,
> From the earth, from the hills, from the sky,
> All is well,
> Safely rest,
> God is nigh.

Through all the fun, the meals punctuated by song, the shared interests and delights, even the irritations, we knew that we were united in loyalty to the best and highest that we could imagine. And the daily Bible study was a chance to stretch our imaginations to glimpse what Jesus meant when he talked about the Kingdom of Heaven. For ten days we tasted the sweetness of the presence of God.

But it was while we were still at camp that the blow fell. Marjorie naturally had been elected chief camper, and Jessie Macpherson invited her to go in August on a scholarship to represent Ontario at a camp in Wisconsin. Goodbye to our adventure! I wrote my grief when I got home.

"In my heart I was almost praying that her family

wouldn't let her go although I tried so hard to be unselfish
and wish that they would for her sake. I think the hardest
thing I have ever done is urging her to go. We had a long
walk yesterday. Mother of course is disgusted, especially
whenever she thought of the job teaching swimming that
I had turned down, and when Marjorie came up Mother
told her how mean she thought it was. I couldn't stop her
but I feel very badly about it. Poor M. Every time I
wanted to say something I'd cry and not be able to speak.
I only hope M is big enough to forgive Mother and forget
it if she can."

Marjorie went off to Wisconsin, and I wrote to her
instead of writing in my diary. As always, she understood
and shared. "That first dear letter of hers is more precious
than I can express." Added to my disappointment about
our week together, I was suffering from camp-sickness,
the inevitable let-down after the high experience. I
thought constantly about Normandale, reliving the days.
I couldn't talk to Mother about it. I already sensed her
resentment at the emotional attachment I was feeling for
Jessie Macpherson and the far horizons she had shown
me.

But I knew I could not keep to myself the vision I had
found there, and I began to plan to introduce CGIT at St.
Aidan's. When I had been in Grade Eleven and only
thirteen years old, I had become bored by Sunday school
and had asked the rector, Dr. Cotton, if I could have one
of the junior classes to teach. Faced with the challenge of
teaching, I began to study the Bible and the lesson out-
lines seriously and to develop convictions. At seventeen,
after my second summer as a camper, I was able to get
Dr. Cotton's permission to invite my Sunday-school class

to become a CGIT group. There were about ten girls in it, boisterous, giggling, irresponsible twelve-year-olds, with one or two a bit older, and Madeline Glenn who had sneaked in under the age line at eleven. Barbara Lunn was the natural leader in the group, and the first president. She giggled like the others but was mature enough to understand the goals: "Under the leadership of Christ to cherish health, seek truth, know God, and serve others."

I look back on the first three years of our group life as a hectic time in which Tuesday evening came rushing along with unnatural frequency. It was always Tuesday evening! And that meant a dash through dinner, a hasty gathering-up of equipment, and a fast walk down to the church, the straggling in of those who happened to turn up that night, an hour of shrieking "fun" playing basketball in the gym, and eventually Barbara's attempts to settle them down for a discussion of whatever was on the agenda. We called ourselves Shawnees, an Indian word for silverbirch, in complement to Silverbirch Avenue where the church was situated. The Shawnees put on plays, ran mother-and-daughter banquets, sold hyacinths to raise money for the church, went carolling at Christmas, hiked along the beach of a Sunday morning to cook a shore breakfast, and did many less memorable things. The program was based on the project method, which demanded that the girls themselves plan, carry out, and then evaluate their activities, and I was young enough to take such a pattern seriously. It was a washed-out dishrag that trailed back up the hill after those meetings.

One evening in the spring of our third year, someone, who may have been sick of hearing me talk about

Normandale, suggested that we could have a camp of our own on the May 24th holiday. Marg Cook offered to ask her parents if we could borrow their cottage at Orr Lake about eighty miles north of Toronto. Someone else knew a man who worked for a lumber company and might have a truck that could take us up there. We began talking budgets and menus, amid many hilarious suggestions for cost-cutting, and went on to list the equipment needed and personal packing "musts." Suddenly it was time to go home. Next Tuesday couldn't come too quickly. The parents trusted me by this time and were co-operative. I was strict about keeping camp out of our Sunday Bible-study sessions, but we sat around afterwards talking over the plans.

Fifty years later we still laugh over the discovery that the bundle big Doris Amson was sitting on in the truck was the bag of bread, now well compacted, and that it was Marg Cook herself who slept alone in the one big bed in the cottage, while the rest of us took turns on the cots and the floor. We sang all the way up, most of the time there, and again on the long bumpy drive home. And when we met again on Tuesday next we hugged one another and laughed and discovered that we had become a real group at last. Camp had done in a weekend what three years of my hard work had never quite accomplished. True to schedule, we then sat down together to evaluate the weekend, which meant going over the details again, giggling at the way things had happened, planning the improvements we wanted next time, and parting good friends.

I made my own list of pros and cons and learned my own lessons. Group leadership taught me some truths that I have lived by ever since. I realized that because I had known what I wanted, in this case to pass on to younger girls the inspiration and happiness I had found for myself in CGIT, I had accepted the drudgery and the discipline that were necessary to achieve it. I never asked myself on Tuesday morning if I really wanted to go down to the church that night. I just went. And I had no idea at the time how rich the rewards to them and to me would be. I believe now that if the goal is worth while it is never fully reached, but I have found that working with dedication towards an end that you believe in is abundant life, happiness enough for anyone. My talent or lack of it is not my responsibility. What is my responsibility is to use what I have to the full.

The camp at Orr Lake was the first in a long series of weekend camps in many different places. One early camp was held on the edge of Scarborough Bluffs when I was a green driver with my first car. Turning too sharply into the laneway to the camp I put the front wheel over the culvert across the ditch. The poor little car hung there, one wheel in space. But co-operation is the essence of group life and even teen-aged girls, if there are enough of them, can lift the front end of a car and put it back on the road. They can have a lot of fun doing it and teasing the clumsy driver. Having rescued the car, we unpacked and made camp. Later in the day Betty Priestly's father drove his daughter out; turning into the laneway, he did the same thing and ended with one wheel hanging over the ditch. None of us will ever forget the look on his face when the girls came running from all directions and without pause or consultation lifted him in his car back onto the road.

Once we had become campers, I knew the joys of
leadership and had few of the headaches. The girls were
eager for Tuesday night, and attendance was steady. As
the years went by the older girls graduated, became
leaders themselves, and formed groups of the younger
teen-agers at the church. The weekend camp in May
became an annual event that included the younger
groups, growing until there were more than fifty girls and
four or five leaders. We did our share in interchurch
activities, and many of us went on to provincial leadership
camps, Beausoleil Island in Georgian Bay or Beau Rivage
among the islands in the St. Lawrence. What a pleasure
to wake up in a bedding roll under the trees, to sit up and
see across the grass the tousled heads of Edie and Madeline, two of my own "children," emerging from their
bedding rolls, ready for another day of the shared heights.

In the early Twenties campers sang popular songs or
parodies of popular songs, pretty shoddy stuff. Jessie
Macpherson changed that. Tall Jessie with her fair hair
cut short, her middy with a dark tie knotted low, her
smiling blue eyes, was "Big Chief" to a generation of girls,
and she cared about quality in music. It was at
Normandale in the shack that I first heard Debussy. The
camp sat spellbound while Elinor Smith, one of us, played
"Minstrels" and "Prélude à l'après-midi d'un faune" on
the camp piano. Jessie taught us folk songs, Negro spirituals, sea chanteys, and songs from other countries,
anything that was singable and of good quality. And we
learned to sing them instead of shouting. The evolution

in music worked upwards into the universities as campers graduated from high school and moved on. By the time Jessie became the innovative and adventurous dean of women at Victoria College of the University of Toronto, she had already revolutionized undergraduate singsongs.

But by far the most important cross-fertilization was an influence that came from the university down into CGIT. It was as a student at U of T that Jessie had come into contact with the leaders and most creative thinkers in the Student Christian Movement. Religious thought in the university and beyond was in ferment. Dr. Salem Bland, whose portrait by Lawren Harris is one of the treasures of the Art Gallery of Ontario, was the minister of Bond Street Church and was inspiring or scandalizing the city with his radical Christianity. Professor James Hooke at Victoria College was challenging his classes and was condemned in the press for poisoning the student mind, which inspired Dave Ketchum, one of the alleged victims, to compose the song "Poisoning the Student Mind."

> Poisoning the student mind,
> Bold me, bad men,
> Villains double-dyed,
> With spiritual arsenic,
> Moral cyanide,
> Are poisoning the student mind!

Every summer Dr. Henry Burton Sharman from the University of Chicago gathered about him at Minnesing Lodge in Algonquin Park a group of students from across Canada to give the New Testament the kind of close

textual examination that was becoming common in literary criticism. He asked the young people to leave their
theological ideas at the door and read the Gospel stories
with an open mind. He had published *Records of the Life of
Jesus*, a harmony of the Gospels, in which there were
three separate columns side by side showing the different
versions of an incident or teaching as found in each of the
three Synoptic Gospels. This facilitated comparison and
invited inquiry. He had also published *Jesus in the Records*
in 1926, a study guide that posed searching questions and
provided no answers. Dr. Sharman was an original and
inspiring teacher who shook up the thinking of a generation of university students and of the younger people
who came under their influence.

Sharman's books and methods were used in the camp
study groups. We had to find our answers in the texts, to
compare the accounts of the life of Jesus in the four
gospels, and to ask why they were sometimes the same
and sometimes different. I began to realize how it was
that the disciples, ordinary, rough workingmen, Jews,
who had met Jesus and gotten to know him as a man,
came to believe that he was more than that, quite unlike
what they had expected in a messiah and yet the true
fulfilment of all their hopes. For the first time in my life I
understood how the disciples and the early church had
struggled to find words to say what they had come to feel
about Jesus. After meeting Jesus the man I could return
to the language of the church and find it full of meaning.
Even the theological words of the creed made sense,
especially with some judicious personal reinterpretation.
Miracles had always been difficulties. I remember the

liberation I experienced the day that Jessie, discussing the feeding of the five thousand, admitted to us that she thought it quite possible that after the young lad offered his loaves of bread and five small fishes, everyone dug into his pocket and pulled out the bit of cheese, the fruit, the leg of chicken, or whatever was buried there, and that the real miracle was the joyful sharing that Jesus inspired. Just as when he said to the Sea of Galilee, "Peace, be still," it was the panic of the disciples that subsided and they remembered afterwards simply a sudden stillness of the waves.

This was the new light that I wanted for the CGIT girls at St. Aidan's, new light that each of them had to find for herself through her own questions and her own search for answers. Weekly Bible study offered the opportunity. The great additional gift of the camps was the release from the distractions and pressures of normal family living, the concentrated focus possible, and a way to express the emotion that developed, to ritualize the love and security that we felt in the camp circle.

One ceremony that was used very often on the last night of camp was a torchlight service, with fire as a symbol of God's spirit. At the end of the day, after the singsong, the games, and the final announcements, each camper was given a bullrush torch that had been dipped in coal oil. The first one was lit from the central campfire, and carried back to the circle to light the next, and the light passed from torch to torch, while we sang the first verses of the hymn "O Love That Wilt Not Let Me Go." We were a flame-brightened circle of earnest faces against the night.

O Light that followest all my way,
I yield my flickering torch to Thee;
My heart restores its borrowed ray,
That in Thy sunshine's blaze its day
May brighter, fairer be.

As this verse was being sung each camper in turn laid
her torch back on the central fire, and the circle joined
hands for the last time to sing taps.

The drop from the heights into real life after camp was
harsh. But I carried the experience inside me as a strength
to help me meet all the less loving encounters, the untidy
frustrations, the irritations of daily living. Every camper
who had shared the exaltation was a friend, reassuring
proof that the hilltop had been as real as the roughness of
the lower road. We wrote to one another, we met at
city-wide CGIT vesper services at Christmas, we went on
hikes in small groups or gathered in planned reunions.
And as soon as we were singing together we were recap-
turing the fellowship and renewing the dedication. I think
the greatest poverty of my life today is that the people I
love and enjoy do not sing it with me.

6

Revelation

HIGH SCHOOL AT MALVERN was a rich experience for me in most ways. The academic work was stimulating and my consistent high marks were gratifying. Outside class Marjorie and I were very much together, active in drama and the literary society and in producing the school magazine. I had other interests that were broadening my horizons. During the last winter at Malvern I travelled by streetcar two nights a week up to Central Technical School to qualify for my bronze and silver medals in swimming and life-saving, studying Latin en route.

And I went every Saturday morning to the Ontario College of Art to what was called the Junior Course, a sort of introductory experience for high school students. At Malvern, art had proved to be a total loss. I hoped at last to learn something about it. The college was a two-storey pink brick building beside the old Grange House in a park at the head of John Street, a bit north of Queen and a mile west of the centre of the city. It had been designed with a shallow gable in a Georgian style to conform to the architecture of the old Baldwin mansion, which was now the art gallery. Both college and gallery were founded by the same artists who had organized the Ontario Society of Artists, but they had been given autonomy from the parent society. Fred Haines, whom I remember as a genial man and a good traditional landscape painter, was president of the society and director of the gallery. George Reid, another fine organizer and a genre painter of great reputation, was principal of the college.

The main thing I learned on those Saturday mornings was that Canadian art was changing, and that there were painters who were pioneering a new style of landscape painting: the Group of Seven. Students, including those of the Junior Course, were admitted free to the Toronto Art Gallery, and we spent hours there becoming familiar with the names and works of all the artists in the annual exhibitions of the Ontario Society of Artists, the Royal Canadian Academy, and the recently formed water-colour society. I became so convinced of the importance of this new direction in Canadian art that I entered the Malvern senior oratorical contest, planning to tell the school about it. To my chagrin there were too few entrants, and the contest was called off.

I doubt that any of the staff at the college tried to teach us anything in the classes on Saturday mornings. They were talent-spotting. We were encouraged rather than taught, which I found disappointing. The only light I gained from those sessions was an understanding of the difference between warm and cool colour. Grace

Coombs, who was left in charge of the class after Arthur
Lismer had given us the pep talk of the day, suggested to
me that the grey I had used in an illustration of the Pied
Piper of Hamlin was "too cool." I showed my bewilder-
ment, and she explained that colours such as red, orange,
and yellow on one side of the spectrum were called warm,
and the blues and greens were known as cool. To warm
up a grey I should mix in a little orange. Welcome my first
fragment of professional vocabulary!

Miss Coombs was a mousy little woman, small and
grey herself, but alert and intelligent. I learned to respect
and like her. Arthur Lismer was the tall, untidy, tweedy
figure in charge of the course. His thin front hair escaped
from the balding spot it was supposed to cover and stuck
straight up when he became excited. He gave us a short
talk at the beginning of every class, setting a project for
the day, teasing us with ironic jokes and irritating me very
much. I wanted him to be serious and to teach us something.

At the end of the term, early in May, the college held
an assembly for all the students and their parents and
friends, at which time the walls were hung with the best
work of the year, and the results announced. I was hoping
to be one of the Juniors chosen to take a second year of
Saturday-morning classes. Mother and Dad came with
me, gratified to hear that two of my paintings had been
chosen to go up on the wall. I was proud to be showing
my new world to my parents as we walked up the broad
path through Grange Park to the college. It was a warm
spring evening with the elms in the park just showing
their first green.

From the front door we were directed to the upstairs

drawing studio, where the plaster statues of Venus and
Hercules and the others had been pushed back against
the wall and the shabby old wooden chairs arranged in
neat rows. We were early (a McCarthy trait) and chose
seats close to the front. Before long the room was full,
with students and even some parents standing against the
wall at the back. Principal Reid welcomed the guests with
a rather prosy speech. Then Arthur Lismer, who was
vice-principal, talked about the Saturday-morning
classes and made characteristic sly jokes about young
people becoming artists. He went on to announce that the
one full-time day scholarship had been won by Miss
Doris McCarthy. I sat there stunned. I don't know what
was done or said for the rest of the evening.

Mother and Dad were pleased but somewhat taken
aback. They accepted me as talented, but we had all
expected that I would go on to university and teach
English in a high school, perhaps writing eventually.
Since at fifteen I was still too young to enter that stream,
next year had been a big question mark. By the end of the
long streetcar ride home to the Beach, the decision had
been made that I was to go to the art college in the fall.

"October 8, 1926: We are actually started. I seem to be
getting along quite famously so far. I love my teachers.
Mr. Lismer is just the same – perhaps a little less odious
in his jokes, but he hasn't lost his baffling attitude of being
amused at the whole world and at us in particular . . . I
don't seem to see any prospects of a kindred spirit."

"October 23: M and I went for a walk out the Kingston
Road and walked past the little house I sketched last
spring up to the railway crossing, and there we settled in
the lovely grassy field just east of the road to Dentonia

Park. We lay in the crisp brown grass and looked at the sky and dreamed that it was spring – and every once in a while we would jump up and wave at a train as it passed. I was telling her all about the students' supper last night when I sat beside Mr. Lismer and suffered horribly from nerves at having him help me to butter and potatoes. But it was quite thrilling watching him draw Mr. [Emanuel] Hahn, who was right opposite me, on the tablecloth. It was so jolly and informal. Mr. Lismer had us in fits with his jokes (e.g. celery – sellery). He has a remarkable brain for seizing puns and can never resist them. But he fascinates me. I love to watch and listen to him talk. His little eyes are so beady and when he makes a joke they peer this way and that and twinkle to see if we're laughing."

"November 19, 1926: I have never been so happy in my life – every minute is just another beautiful deep gratitude. Surely nobody in all the world has as much, so full a life as I. I love Monday – because Mr. Lismer usually gives us a criticism and sometimes a lecture. I love Tuesday – because it's modelling with Mr. Hahn. I'm wild about Wednesday because Mr. Lismer gives us such wonderful lectures, and Museum study is opening a new world of ideas and ecstasy to me, and I always have a nice walk with Tilly [Cowan, another first-year student] – and an extra sleep in the morning [the museum didn't open until 9:30].

"I love Thursdays – because we have modelling again. Friday is the climax of the week because we have our happiest drawing classes and then Composition – the finale – the most looked-forward-to period of the week, when we have wonderful lectures, and both Miss Coombs and Miss Patterson! Then best of all the students' suppers, with Mr. Lismer's silly clever jokes and his humour and friendliness – and Mr. Hahn's geniality and Mr. Stansfield's giggle – and poor John's feeble speeches and of course lots to eat." John Byers was president of the students' club, chairman ex officio.

There was an older woman in the first year with us, Edna Breithaupt, from Kitchener. She offered her cottage on the Grand River near Kitchener as a headquarters for a sketching house party at the end of term. About twelve of us were able to go, and we engaged Yvonne McKague to be our resident teacher. She was Arthur Lismer's assistant at the college, and one of those rare people whose presence turns the lights on. Red-haired, and with the temperament that is supposed to go with that, she gave vitality and laughter to the fortnight.

Before the Kitchener trip we were shocked by the news of Lismer's resignation from the college. The tension between him and George Reid was no secret, and now it had become intolerable. The Kitchener gang, encouraged by Edna Breithaupt, decided that without him the college would be hollow, and that they would rather have his teaching than everything else the school offered. They formed themselves into the Toronto Art Students' League, rented a small house that stood in the corner of Grange Park, and planned for the following year a regime of self-run classes. Lismer agreed to provide some supervision, and Lawren Harris and A.Y. Jackson promised them an occasional criticism.

I longed to be with them. I had won further scholarships, complete tuition for the following year, but my heart was with the league. Dad and I talked it over. He left me to make the decision but helped me to realize that if I ever wanted to teach art in the school system, my degree from the college would be important. I went back to carry on with my course, feeling that the life had gone out of my world.

But I had not known that Ethel Curry would be appearing at the college and entering the second year. She was a dark wisp of a girl from Haliburton, eight years older than I, quiet, self-contained, a "lass with a delicate air," beautiful. We became friends. She had interrupted her art course to teach school in Haliburton for a few years in order to earn some money. Now she was living in an upstairs front room in an old house on St. George Street, a ten-minute walk from the college.

She had a talent for home-making. A fire in the Victorian fireplace, the rented furniture transformed with coloured throws and cushions, candles and flowers, made it a favourite gathering place for the serious students. Too many of our classmates seemed to have little sense of responsibility and were content to fritter away the days, but there were some hard-working, creative people with us, and we began to do things together after class. Ed Noffke from Ottawa, who had been my main rival for first place in each subject the year before, was one of the regulars. Two lads from China became our good companions. Ruth Dingle from Montreal made fun wherever she was. And there was tall red-haired Franklin Casey, whose blue eyes looked off into space and who wrote and read poetry. Three or four of us would go to a play at the Royal Alexandra, taking the cheapest seats, or sometimes walk together up to Convocation Hall at the university for a late-afternoon free organ recital, and back to Curry's for sandwiches and coffee. To my mind the name Curry suited her better than Ethel, and increasingly we all called her that.

One day Herbie Stansfield (as we disrespectfully thought of him), the man who was supposed to teach us applied design, told us about a production of *Porgy* at the Princess Theatre on Adelaide Street and urged us to see it. We trooped down and were completely spellbound. It was an all-black cast, very well presented and acted, with much singing even in this dramatic version, which preceded the musical. The scene of the wake in the upper room was lit by a lantern on the floor, and the gaunt figures of the wailing mourners were exaggerated in the huge shadows that swung from side to side on the back wall in rhythm with the singing. I came out of the theatre dazed, unable to grasp that I was back in Toronto on familiar Adelaide Street. For this I forgive Mr. Stansfield for two years of dull, useless classes.

The name of his course was enough to condemn it. Design was thought of at the college as something applied to a useful object in order to make it visually appealing. We were taught to make lampshades, with stencilled patterns as adornments. This was at the time that the Bauhaus School in Germany was revolutionizing the concept of design and preaching functionalism. This fresh air had not yet reached Toronto.

I don't know whom to blame for the fact that I survived four years of instruction in sculpture and was given high marks, without learning to think structurally. When modelling a head from life I kept turning the clay round and round on the stand to compare its silhouette with the corresponding view of the model. I thought two-dimensionally. And I confused two-dimensional copying with truth to life.

J.W. Beatty's Saturday-morning classes in composition were good, although he was so steeped in the nineteenth century that the subjects he gave us were usually Biblical stories with masses of figures in them. At least we were challenged to think about arrangement, focus, centre of interest, and relationships of scale.

This was the year that Charles Goldhamer, a recent graduate, was hired back as an instructor in still life and costume painting in water-colour. He had been well grounded by Arthur Lismer, and he taught us to use a full brush and put the paint on with courage and decision.

A remarkable feature of the College of Art in those pre-expansion days was the basement lunch-room, where Mrs. Merrill, the matronly white-haired woman with the pleasant smile, made pies that are still unrivalled in my experience. It was characteristic of her that, when she learned that one of the students had had a brush with tuberculosis, she began to boil all the cutlery to protect the rest of us. She fed fifty or more of us every Friday night with a good hot meal and a choice of her pies, and I never once heard her scold.

The big social event of every year was the college masquerade for which the student committee in charge, working with a different staff member each year, chose a theme or historical period. In my first year the choice was the court of King Arthur, and everyone was expected to contrive some sort of medieval dress to wear. We turned the largest of the studios upstairs into a castle, and I had my first lesson in stage painting and masonry as I helped to cover the walls with stonework, each stone subtly highlighted and shadowed to give it dimension, and the pointing done with enough but not too much care. The senior students produced wonderful heraldic banners, shields, and tapestries. Another by-product of the masquerades was that we learned to recognize the difference between the students who took the last afternoon off to have their hair done or work on their costumes and those who stayed to finish the job and even to sweep up and wax the floors for dancing.

The next year Curry invited me to spend the Christmas holidays painting with her at Haliburton, and with Mother's and Dad's co-operation it was decided that I should take the train up the day after Christmas. What an experience! I changed at Lindsay to a mixed train, one passenger coach and a couple of freight cars, which ambled up the track, stopping for leisurely unloading at funny little stations and even at crossroads. Although I had left the Danforth station before nine, by noon we were only at Kinmount, hardly a hundred miles on our way. The conductor-cum-trainman-cum-baggageman advised me where I could get some lunch in the village. While I was still eating my boiled egg there, he sent a youngster to tell me that the train was ready to leave "whenever you have finished, Miss."

It was dark when we reached Haliburton. I emerged from the smelly coach with its dim oil lamps into a world of sharp cold snow and brilliant stars. Waiting for me was a horse and sleigh, with Curry's mother, a round bundle of shabby fur coat below a woollen bonnet, perched on the driver's seat.

It was like stepping back fifty years. The Curry house had electric light, but water was gravity-fed from a cistern upstairs, which had to be filled by a hand pump in the kitchen. Too enthusiastic an attack at the pump brought water pouring down the kitchen wall from above. Hung up in the back shed was the frozen carcass of a buck, shot in hunting season, ready for butchering piece by piece as needed. Down in the cellar was the wood furnace, and the long wall of cut wood to keep it fed. Curry and I made a work space there, with our backs kept warm by the furnace, and a strong blue bulb hung from the ceiling to give us "daylight" for finishing the oil panels that we brought home every morning and afternoon. Besides the wood in the cellar was an incredible collection of rubber boots, overshoes, old coats, and sweaters, mittens, hoods, scarves, and snowshoes. If we needed something, we just looked for it. It was there.

Curry's father, known as W.R., was a man of parts, owner of the only garage in town, reeve of the village, local undertaker, district inspector of roads, owner-manager of the livery stable that provided horses for the doctor and for anyone else who needed winter transportation, and above all a gentle man, at home in the woods, in the kitchen, at the hockey rink, and at the dance at the town hall on New Year's Eve. Curry told me that when she was a very small girl, her mother and father had moved from Irondale to Haliburton, travelling down river by raft. The family and all the household goods were piled on it, including the cow. Mr. Curry had worked before that as a cook in a lumber camp. He was a marvel-

lous example of first-generation capitalism, from rags to
leading citizen of Haliburton by imagination and hard
work.

The night after I arrived in Haliburton I was introduced to square dancing with a genuine resident fiddler
and a procession of good-looking young lads whom
Curry identified as the former primary grade children she
had taught in her first days as a public-school teacher.

Curry gave me her world, the winter woods full of
animal tracks, the snow fanning from the stump fences in
drifts of sculptural purity, the log homes and the tar-paper
shacks with blue wood smoke in curls above them. I had
the wooden sketch box I had used at Kitchener, although
I had to learn a new way of using it for working out of
doors in the winter. Curry taught me to lay out my palette
before I went out, squeezing my colours onto the floor of
the box, white at the corner, the warm colours in spectrum order across the top, the cool colours down the left
side (for us right-handed artists). Besides the practical
advantage of avoiding accidental mixes, it was pleasant
to see the hues in logical sequence. The narrow partition
across the front kept my brushes and turps cup separated
from the palette part of the box. In those days I was still
using hog's-hair brushes, stiff-bristled and square-ended,
from a quarter of an inch to a full inch in width. Having
heard Mr. Lismer jeer about people who used one-haired
brushes, I avoided very small ones. I was painting on
wood, usually panels of poplar because it was a wood
without an aggressive grain. I shellacked them to prevent
the wood from leeching the oil out of the paint, and the
shellac gave me a warm light colour to paint over. And I
placed my opened sketch box between my legs at arm's

length so that it was necessary to hold the brush by the end of the handle and draw with wrist movement, not with my fingers. I watched Curry and learned from her.

We found our subjects in the village itself, along the river, down at the sawmill, or out on the frozen lake looking back at the hills. I was composing as I had been taught, choosing a focus of interest, a building or a part of a building, the pattern made by the open water in a snow-bordered stream, a hillside broken up by contrasting areas of evergreen trees and the grey purple-pink of bare maple woods. After I had drawn my composition in a thin turps wash I would begin to paint it, as directly as possible, putting down a firm stroke of colour and not messing it around afterwards, letting distance blend the brush strokes and clarify the story. We painted every day all day, usually within walking distance of home.

But not always. "December 29: The end of a perfect day. It began fairly early with the words 'sleigh ride,' which woke me with a jump. Curry and I dressed and ate hastily, and then packed into the cutter, too stuffed and bundled for action of any kind. I loved the motion of the horses, the crispness and tingle of the air, and the sideways skidding of the sleigh, up slowly, along smartly, bells jingling – nose running, mind happy – playing with loving thoughts of Marjorie and Jessie Mac.

"We saw some striking bits of colour – a blue door, and a pink-and-grey one, and some gay washings hung out to dry. The last few miles were through a wild bit of wood – rough uneven trail, hardly a road – twining black birches and elms tangled up in saplings and underbrush. There were three patches where the road was sunk in black bog and the horses would hardly take the jump across. I

thought that the sleigh would break and deposit us in the
mud or else that it would stick there forever. Arriving at
camp [one of Mr. Curry's lumber camps] was an adventure too. We sat down at one of the long tables and ate
gustily from tin plates, drinking out of tin bowls. But the
climax, more thrilling even than the cutter part, was the
walk over the lake, dazzling in sunlight, Curry and the
men ahead, picturesque in breeches and windbreakers,
casting vivid shadows, and the hills around the lake. I
loved the keen wind, the feel of the snow under my feet,
and especially the sense of high adventure.

"Then for the drive home I cuddled low against Curry,
casting a submerged eye over the rugs at the heavenly
colour: bright mauve sunlight on hills, a wonderful after-
glow – Venus, and later Mars and Jupiter – golden light
on trees, a barn with the bright sky shining through."

"January 2, 1929: Yesterday it snowed heavily and left
the village in a quiet hush – all contours softened, all
harshness covered, only a brooding peace and mystery.
Our walk to the rink was indescribably lovely. The stars
in a black-blue sky were brighter than ever before – and
the street-lights made circles of cold yellow light, ac-
cented by the tenderly blue-purple shadows between
them. Footprints across the snow made me ache with
their beauty. Every step sent a little shower of powdery
flakes into the air. The blacksmith's shop was a perfect
composition – dark against a still darker sky, roof and
snow gleaming dimly, and a lovely pattern of light, fan-
shaped on the snow from the two windows in the front.
It was twenty-five below zero, so cold that my nose
twitched and was stiff, and our breath froze in white frost
on our hair. The stars were bright and the smoke rose

quietly straight up, meeting as it slowly spread into one smoky pall that caught the light from the lamps and gave a solemn cold look to the village – and the snow squeaked and crackled underneath us."

And so back to school in Toronto to start 1929. J.W. Beatty was the instructor in "life," both drawing and painting. This meant working from a nude model. When I had first heard – up at Muskoka, from an art student who was staying on another island – that artists' models didn't wear clothes, I was unable to imagine that such a thing could be possible, that someone could stand up in front of other people with nothing on and be looked at! Marjorie and I were so modest, even with each other, that when we took skinny dips in those days we crept to the water under cover of darkness, wrapped in raincoats, and didn't peek. But by the time I was in third year, ready for life classes, we had all become so accustomed to seeing the drawings and paintings up on the wall that there was little sensation.

Mr. Beatty was a stocky, middle-aged man with thinning grey hair, a chain smoker, with a wheeze that made talking sometimes difficult. His fingers were yellow-brown from nicotine and shook so that you wondered if he could aim at the page when he sat beside you to give a criticism. But once on the paper, his hand was in control, and his line confident and true. He was a remarkable man who had been a fireman and had taught himself to draw from plaster casts in the fire station while the other boys were playing their eternal bridge or poker. Later he studied in Paris and became a competent academic painter, fairly well respected in the community. But his heart was full of bitterness towards those artists who received more recognition than he had, and he hated – it is not too strong a word – the men who were challenging the academic standards of the nineteenth century, and especially he hated the Group of Seven in Canada. Lismer was no longer at the college, but gentle J.E.H. MacDonald – of the curly red hair and the voice that broke in a squeak – was head of design, Franz Johnston was on the staff, and the students were full of admiration for Lawren Harris and A.Y. Jackson. The members of the Group whom I met at the college, at the Art Students' League, or in their own studios, seemed to be warm, generous-minded men, critical of the artists who were still painting Canada as if it were England, but without personal rancour and full of encouragement for the students.

Beatty's work seemed to have stopped progressing, and I felt at the time that his spirit was so warped by anger and resentment that he could never be great as an artist. However, he ran the Port Hope Summer School, a resident hostel for art students, close to the old mill and dam in Port Hope. It was an experience not unlike camp, where the informal comradeship of your fellow artists, the men as well as the women, cemented bonds. Technically, Mr. Beatty had much to teach us, although I share the conviction, experienced by more than one student, that it took years to free yourself from Beatty colour. This was a characteristic over-all look to the work of his students that is difficult to define but easy to recognize. He invented and popularized the light wooden sketch box that I used in Haliburton, the model in which the floor of the box was the palette and the lid a sketching panel held by grooves in the sides. It took eight-and-a-half by ten-and-a-half-inch panels. The time came when

I found these too small and Dad made me a similar but larger box, which I used for many years.

It was a great satisfaction to me that Dad took that kind of interest in my schoolwork and was prepared to come to the Friday-night suppers with me on occasion and meet my friends there. Our gang had come to include Narcisse, a French Canadian who had Gallic charm and gallantry, big Ted Drover from Newfoundland, and Oscar, who had a strong Russian accent. Mother looked on them all with deep suspicion, but Dad met them graciously and enjoyed the students as well as the guest speakers at the gatherings.

I was unwilling for that satisfying third year to end, although we looked forward to the final dinner and announcement of results as a high occasion. By this time the triflers had been weeded out. Those who remained were serious students who had behind them months of hard grind and a lot of steam to blow off.

"May 19, 1929: The real gladness came afterwards when we grabbed hands and went leaping along Dundas – laughing and shrieking, and there was the fun of finding a hurdy-gurdy man, and of dancing madly in a circle on the corner of McCaul, and of flinging restraint to the winds and just letting loose – a new experience for me. Skipping up University we stopped around the tulips and smelt them gustily . . . and of course the best bit of the whole evening was coming home with Curry, and falling asleep beside her with scarcely a good night. Thank God for our fourth year still to come, and may there be other times together after it."

7

Tug of War

WHILE PART OF ME was an art student, working hard, learning to see and to draw, another part was a teen-ager exploring the meaning of life and what it meant to be a Christian. After my first year at the college and the Kitchener sketching house party, I went again to Normandale for the first Camp Council, not a normal cross-section of CGIT girls this time, but elected delegates from all parts of Ontario. I was invited as a thank-you for the drawings I had been making for camp folders and other CGIT literature. Camp Council was everything that camp had been before, multiplied and intensified. Jessie Macpherson was the director, with a very strong staff of leaders including her friend Mary Rowell. That summer Jessie lent me her university notes on religious knowledge, and I learned about textual sources of both the Old and New Testaments.

In the late summer of that year, 1927, I went to a

student conference at Elgin House in Muskoka. This was the big yellow frame hotel that we used to see from the *Sagamo* when we took our annual boat trip up the lakes from Silver Island. It was memorable to us for Mother's comment, "There's no smoking or playing cards, but they're full all the time." We chose to pretend that she was accusing the guests of lying around in a drunken stupor. Actually, she was remarking on its popularity in spite of its strongly Methodist flavour. It was a gracious place, not luxurious but comfortable, surrounded by wide lawns on beautiful Lake Joseph, the most northerly of the Muskoka lakes. This was the year of Church Union and ecumenism was in the air, a good enough reason for the hotel's being made available for the annual conferences of the Student Christian Movement.

There, for ten days or so, I was plunged into a more adult version of camp, with university students from across Canada, and leaders from around the world. Gregory Vlastos, Reinhold Niebuhr, Murray Brooks and Gertrude Rutherford, Dr. Marion Hilliard, King Gordon, John Low and John Line, Dr. Ernest Thomas and his beautiful black-haired daughter, Isabel, are some of the names that come back to me, but I cannot be sure of which years had which leaders. I felt very young, but I watched, and I listened. Elgin House conferences were valuable, never as intense for me as Camp Council, but intellectually challenging, demanding that I face difficult problems of international suspicion, racism, and economic injustice. Art students seldom talked of such things among themselves or seemed to care.

Once back in Toronto I was invited to Sunday-evening study groups with some of the leaders I had met at Elgin

House. One of the men guiding us was the notorious
Professor Hooke, target of some very critical complaints
that had been aired around the university. Of course I
thought he was marvellous, and I was flattered to be
admitted to such sophisticated company. We were studying Alfred North Whitehead's writings, from which I
memorized a definition of God, hoping that by brooding
over it long enough I would understand what it meant.
"God is the actual but non-temporal entity by which the
indeterminateness of mere creativity is transmuted to a
determinate freedom."

I was learning about alternative concepts of truth.
"April 19, 1928: I was at Lawren Harris's studio tonight,
a very interesting experience. His slant on things is
'occult' to put it mildly and amusingly contrasted to Prof.
Hooke's. Of course both he and Prof. Hooke have probably graduated from the necessity of laying hold on
history, facts, and experience, and have grown from them
into a wider understanding of their implications. I'd love
to have him turned loose on the study group at Hooke's."

Of more value to me than the metaphysical talk of the
great ones was a phrase that stuck with me from one of
the Gospels, "Sirs, I would see Jesus." Increasingly, I did.

The Ontario Girls' Work Board was the interdenominational committee with responsibility for CGIT, and Jessie was its provincial secretary. Her office was in the
Methodist Bookroom at 299 Queen Street West, the
handsome pale grey stone building at the corner of John
Street that I passed every morning as I walked from the
streetcar to the college. When I was lucky, Jessie would
be walking down through Grange Park as I was walking
up, and there would be time for a greeting. The Girls'

Work Board used me increasingly as an artist to create
graphics needed for camp folders, leaders' magazines,
and other promotional material.

Both Marjorie and I were involved in youth conferences that were bringing together teen-age girls and boys.
The life of my own CGIT group at St. Aidan's was in full
swing. And there were camp reunions, vesper services,
shore breakfasts, conferences out of town at which I
sometimes had to make speeches or lead in singing and
games. Letters flew back and forth from camp friend to
camp friend, letters full of affection, lighting up the day
when they arrived. I was being pulled in two directions.
I loved school and was happy with Curry and the gang
there, but their friendship was without the spiritual dimension that gave richness to my love for Marjorie and
Jessie and our widening circle of camp friends.

I was tormented by the conflicting demands and delights of these different worlds. "Sunday night, February
17, 1929: I am still in heaven. Reunion was miraculous.
It 'renewed and created faith' – faith in the dearness of
all of them, in the reality of camp loveliness, in Miss
[Mary] Allison's uniqueness. Jessie told us quietly about
Miss Allison's way of complete giving of herself to people,
and later I sat on the arm of Miss Allison's chair, with my
arm around her neck and her head on my shoulder, re-
solving to ask her help in my Big Muddle. A short talk
with Jack Alfsen the other afternoon served to engulf me
deeper in my Doubting Castle. I'm afraid of being convinced that art isn't the path to take – perhaps that might be
worse than hope and misgivings alternately." John Alfsen,
who was a graduate of the college but still hanging around,
had been talking pessimistically about life as an artist.

"February 22: Just had my usual row with Mother about CGIT. For a couple of weeks now it's been nag, nag – about me thinking too much of that and too little of my work. There's something in it, but I'm fed up to the ears with hearing about it. It takes all the bloom off."

"February 26: I've been working hard at school and loving it! Why can't I learn once and for all that the harder I work the happier I am."

My diary is full of the tensions among my three worlds: college, home, and CGIT. Mother was not well. She was having a wretched menopause, labelled "nerves" by the doctors, enduring backaches, nausea, and insomnia. I would listen for her voice in the morning, because its tone told me the kind of day it was going to be for everybody. All the fun had gone out of her. I had never been able to discuss ideas with her and had long since stopped trying, but now there was no pleasing her on any level, and I was both helpless and guilty. Mother's religious convictions were summed up in "Honour thy father and thy mother." She resented my new loyalties.

Marjorie had taken a room uptown to save her energy for study at Victoria College. She was living close to the campus in the house on St. Mary Street that was shared by Jessie and some of the other Girls' Work secretaries.

"M came home today. I constantly rebel at her being away, and I hated her little adventures with Miss Allison and Jessie and Avis Marshall – but mostly I hated myself for hating them. All day I have been tired out – worn right down, and discovering myself weeping in corners. I think that jealousy is probably at the bottom of the whole matter."

"March 27: I'm happy tonight with a queer incredulous

thrill – such a bombshell has been thrown into my static world. This afternoon walking through Queen's Park with Jessie, she said, 'I wish you were two years older. Oh, I guess I don't either – but if you were two years older I could leave you my job.' I laughed at her – of all the stupendous and absurd ideas. Poor Ontario if I were. 'Don't be funny, Jessie!' 'I'm not being funny. I mean it. I'd be quite willing to trust you with it.' And she asked me, as Miss Allison had half asked me before, if I would consider Girls' Work as a profession. Wish I could answer that question to myself."

In the spring of that year I was offered a job teaching crafts at one of the private all-summer camps. These camps were well established, well run, and expensive, attracting girls from affluent families and able to pay their leaders. But they were secular. "I've been weighing the pros and cons with M and Mother, and I'll see Jessie perhaps tomorrow and ask her what she thinks about it. I rebel at the amount I should have to give up: Beausoleil [a CGIT leadership camp], two weeks at Port Hope Summer School, July at the cottage with Dad – and to weigh against all that there is $100, useful experience, and some very hard work."

"April 25: More complications, and still more golden dreams. Jessie offered me the directorship of county camps. My heart instantly says yes. Dad says if you would rather, by all means. Mother says a good deal more, with much emphasis and exasperation. To her eyes I am throwing away a wonderful opportunity to make good contacts, fair money, and some experience – all for nothing. But my heart sings loudly."

A county camp was a ten-day CGIT camp with the site,

leaders, cook, and so on provided by the local organization, and the director sent in by the provincial Girls' Work
Board to ensure that the camp met CGIT standards. As
director I would receive transportation, my keep, and a
ten-dollar honorarium per camp, and I would be responsible for the program, discipline, security, and smooth
operation of everything except the finances. It would be
my camp. After several days of dithering, torn between
my own wishes and Mother's arguments, which had some
merit, I offered to take the all-summer camp position if
the salary were raised to $150. There followed two weeks
of suspense, in which I wondered at my temerity at
considering a job teaching crafts, all of which I should
have to learn before I could teach them. But my bluff was
not called. It was decided that the commercial camp's
budget did not allow for such a high salary.

"April 29: Praise be! It's county camps – and I'm
thrilled!"

This was the same spring that Doug sold his savings
bond and bought a ring for Audrey Dale, whom we
hardly knew, but who was on the other end of the line
when Doug was closeted upstairs with the telephone in
Mother's bedroom for an hour at a time. Doug's telephone conversations through the years had been a family
joke: monosyllabic, one or two grunts and an infrequent
"okay." We had realized that only love could have
changed him so much. He would be graduating as an
engineer in a month, and in another year – marriage? Ken
and Betty had already been married for a year and were
expecting their first child. They were living in Ohio
where Ken had gone for post-graduate study in anaesthe-

sia. I would soon be the only young McCarthy at home.

Someone else was in love that spring. Roy Wood was at Victoria College with Marjorie. He was one of the undergraduates who took her to the proms, to concerts, and anywhere else he could persuade her to let him escort her. She was friendly but not interested. "Poor Roy. He loves her – and she's filling his whole life without her caring at all about him. I can see his point of view so plainly that I'm sorry for him."

Curry too confided to me one day, when we were lying on the grass in Grange Park, looking at crocuses, that she had been engaged for three years and was to have been married by now but that he had ditched her. "I'm not over it yet so I don't talk about it. You needn't fear for my health. It's my sanity. That's why I get so dreadfully blue sometimes." I looked at her with new concern and new sympathy.

Two weeks later she told me that the man was in Toronto and going to the same parties as some of the college gang.

"May 16, 1930: With Curry to the Conservatory [of Music] at noon today, and plump into Him, with a wonderful smile. No wonder poor Curry feels as she does. When we escaped, she grabbed me and we walked, hard. And she told me about raking out her whole gallery of newspaper clippings of him last night, and of waking up this morning to find them all over the floor staring at her."

Curry was to live through a dozen more years at the mercy of her love for this man. He turned up in her life, enjoyed her forgiveness, raised her hopes, dashed them again, not once but over and over. He had charm, good

looks, talent, and no conscience. I'm sure that he found
Curry's generosity flattering. I wish he could have known
what her friends thought of him.

While love raged around me in one form or another, I
remained unscathed, interested in an academic way, but
waiting until I met the Right Man. Those at the college
were friends, and I enjoyed playing and working with
them, but there was nothing romantic between us.

"May 10, 1930: Tonight was our long-promised party
at Mr. [Franz] Johnston's studio – such fun. That gang
are the dearest people and we can laugh and be absurd
with the happiest freedom. I can imagine the impression
of an outsider: Archie in an armchair with Curry – hair
wild – in his arms, and a bottle in his hand; Frances a
lumpy heap on the couch, hair still wilder; Ruth, scanty
of clothes, cavorting; Wen and Les sprawled intimately
on the floor. But the gladness of our fellowship is in its
very freedom – and its frank acceptance of the limitations
of comradeship. I can't help exulting in the contrast
between parties now and what they used to be at high
school."

For the time being I was so happy at the prospect of
directing three county camps, having a painting session
at J.W. Beatty's school at Port Hope and a few weeks at
the cottage with Dad and Mother and Doug's intended,
that my big muddle seemed to have sorted itself out, and
art and CGIT to have achieved peaceful coexistence.

8

Into the World

BEFORE I WAS DUE at my first county camp there was time in the summer of 1929 for two weeks at the Port Hope Summer School. The school had been contrived out of a massive barn with a stone foundation. Upstairs there were small bedrooms for the girls, simply furnished with cots and plain dressers. The boys had their own building close by, and there was a dining room and kitchen on the property, which shelved down to the shingly bank of the Ganaraska River. Just upriver from the school was a dam that made an excellent swimming pool. Its water spilled over to create a boisterous shower bath. A farm a few hundred yards away offered pictur-esque buildings and outbuildings, hay stooks, and an orchard just past its blossom. There were country roads leading north and west and east. South of the school lay the town complete with cottage gardens, little shops, and more pretentious buildings for the ambitious to paint.

We met in the barn studio every morning for class
criticism, with the previous day's work ranged around the
room, leaning against the wall. Mr. Beatty smoked and
wheezed through his comments on the offerings and then
sent us off to find our subjects for the day. If we settled
within sight of the school, he might turn up as we were
working to give some help or direction, or even an occasional demonstration. He was at his best at Port Hope,
genial and interested, and we were careful to avoid rousing his ire by raising any subjects that touched his pet
hates.

The atmosphere was conducive to hard work. Most of
the students were serious and there was no division into
beginners and advanced, so that we learned from the best
among us as well as from the formal instruction. Frances
Anne Johnston and Franklin Arbuckle were both there,
students junior to me, not yet engaged but recognized as
a couple, and already showing promise of the fine artists
they became. Margaret Stevenson was a former nurse
who was the centre of the fun, but quick to notice an
unhappy face and do something about it. She would have
made a marvellous Camp Mother. Frank Casey, whose
poetic detachment still tempted me to romantic daydreams, was a good enough reason for me to get up in the
dark and walk with him a few miles to make a sketch of
the sunrise over Lake Ontario.

There was barely turnaround time before I was off
again. The first county camp took me to New Liskeard,
farther north than I had ever been, eighty miles or so up
the railway line that Dad had built when the family lived
in North Bay and about three hundred miles north of
Toronto. Considering that I was to be in charge of fifty

girls and their ten leaders, it did seem a bit ridiculous that
Mother worried about my making the train trip by myself. I was all eagerness.

"July 17, 1929: After a very wonderful night – the old
half-forgotten happiness of the motion of the train, bells
clanging away into silence as we passed, the moon shining
on my head, little lights that work for me when I want –
a letter to Margaret Stevenson, and a curious inability to
realize that this miraculous camping experience has really
begun. I woke early this morning, shocked to see that
daylight had brought the north, with tar-covered shacks,
many telegraph poles and rocks and spruce."

I was met at the station by a pleasant woman who was
to be Camp Mother. I stayed with her until the next day,
when we were all to be driven the twenty miles or so to
the campsite. My hostess was hanging out a washing that
afternoon, fighting the wind that was whipping the sheets
up and over the line in a mad dance. It was a blue
sparkling exuberant day. "Don't you love a wind like
this?" I asked.

"No," she said. "It frightens me. It was a day just like
this that the forest fire wiped out Haileybury," and I
remembered the terrible disaster to that nearby town in
1922, seven years earlier. The fire sweeping forward on
all sides had levelled the buildings and left six thousand
people homeless, driving them into the lake to escape the
flames and filling the air with such dense smoke that many
died from suffocation.

The wind was still blowing two days later, when we
were settled into camp on Lake Ste. Marie. It was the first
use of the site for camping, and fairly primitive. We ate
in the open, ranged on rough benches along the sides of

trellis tables. The wind was so strong the first morning that the corn flakes blew out of the bowls, and we ended up using mugs, with one hand across the top as a lid. The cook had never been away from her husband before, and she wept quietly but steadily for three days.

My tent-mates were a congenial group: a nurse, a young teacher, and Mrs. Patterson, of the broad Scottish brogue. As she unwound herself from her bedding roll in the morning after the bugle had blown for what we called "upsetting exercises," she would exhort us, "Brothers, let us groan," and we would respond in unison.

We were not always in such agreement. When I found myself with a discipline problem, with three of the girls leading in noisy nonsense after lights out, it was Mrs. Patterson who thought the solution was to put a leader in each tent. But this was against my principles. The only discipline I wanted for the camp was self-discipline. I called a council hour. The camp as a whole was presented with the issue, and the girls agreed that there must be rules, and that they would respect them. The campers asked from each of the three rebels a promise to co-operate. The promises were given, and what is more, they were kept. What had threatened to be a disaster turned into a triumph. For several years afterwards, Katie Frew, the conspicuous ringleader, used to write me at Christmas. I can still see her mischievous eyes and her fly-away black hair.

Before my next assignment, which was a church summer school on Manitoulin Island, there was time for a day's pause at Temagami. This was dramatically beautiful country that I had glimpsed from the train going up. I organized a stopover of one night in the hotel on the

waterfront and spent a happy afternoon sketching near
the edge of the lake. It was the next morning, when I woke
to find one eye swollen shut and my face so lopsided that
I could hardly speak, that I learned that the rather both-
ersome little midges that had been all around me while I
was working were blackflies. Now I know! But it was not
the flies that went into my diary.

"I did a sketch this afternoon from the general store at
Temagami and feel terribly thrilled about it – but even
more thrilled at the interest shown in it by a young chap,
and his tentative approach for purchase. If I could only
sell a sketch – my future would be made! I could feel
justified in the expense this trip is being."

I didn't make a sale that day, but I was able to save a
few dollars on train fare by accepting a ride down to
North Bay from a stranger staying in the hotel. He turned
out to be a groper, and I had a tense, wretched afternoon,
fearful that he might stop the car and become really
importunate. North Bay never looked so good! Sheldon
and Mattie Clement, old friends of the family, were comfort and security when I was dropped at their home to
spend the night before travelling on to Manitoulin Island.
They had shared the North Bay years with the young
McCarthys, and they told me tales of the minstrel shows
that they used to put on, with Mother in blackface as one
of the end men. Sheldon had been Dad's assistant engineer on the railroad construction, and their son, young
Shel, was born the same year as Douglas. By this time I
was old enough to relish these glimpses of my parents
before I had known them.

"Mindemoya, Manitoulin, Sunday morning, August 4:
In the midst of another funny adventure and scared

green. I'm to take the adult class at the Sunday school –
on Daniel – and have neither convictions about Daniel
nor courage to face the class. I'll probably be the youngest
of them. It's a ghastly feeling. And add to that the prospect
of speaking to the whole Sunday school at the close of the
lesson. Whew!

"Yesterday was an unexpected adventure. We had a
very rough passage to the island in a gallant little steamer,
and it rocked and twisted and shook. Waves fifteen feet
high, fifty feet between the crests. I revelled. Each moun-
tainous bank of water would send the little ship almost
on its side, and people turned pea-green around me. Such
fun! But for all its fun I was lonely. Goodness how I
wanted Marjorie or Jessie or Curry or someone to exult
with me. Joy alone is only half joy. Why do my wonderful
adventures of gladness and travel always come apart from
M, and why does her life run away from mine?"

Between the Manitoulin summer school and my next
camp I had barely an hour in Toronto, just time to change
trains. "It was great being met by Mother and Dad and
having a blessed hour with them before it was time to
dash off again. I can never be glad enough for the new
appreciation of them that this year has brought. Dad is
my friend now, my dear, understanding, understood
friend. Today he said that this summer I had been trying
my wings and looked better than he had ever before seen
me look. Dad's life has been given to us in some ways,
and it is for us to give to the world some fruits of the fine
steady honourable quiet life he has lived."

Mother had become used to the idea of my being away
from home, but she never did more than tolerate my

choice of CGIT camps. However, all three of us were
looking forward to the fortnight we would have together
at the end of the summer at "the cabin," as we had named
our own cottage at Beaumaris. Mother had become reconciled to it and even proud of it.

Audrey Dale came with us, giving me a chance to get
to know my sister-in-law-to-be. And Marjorie managed
to get there for a few days. We were both desperate for a
reunion and a chance to share the experiences we had
been having separately. She was just back from two
months at Camp Tanamakoon in Algonquin Park and
was full of its beauty, and of the very different atmosphere
she had found there. Most of the other leaders were
students or graduates of the Margaret Eaton School of
Expression, the organization that had tried in vain to
teach us to be ballet dancers in our youth. It was a camp
that stressed sports and physical perfection, and
Marjorie's function there had been to add a spiritual
dimension to the life. She helped the campers to build an
outdoor chapel and led them in worship. In turn, she was
taught to ride, a skill that stood her in good stead later.

October plunged me back into college. "Another year,
the last. Curry and I look at each other and smile ruefully,
and wonder a little when we say 'last.' Incredible. Such a
short while ago I was looking forward to four whole
years, marvelling, and now I marvel more that they are
gone. Will all of life be like this?"

Sometime during the autumn, Curry and I did a survey
of our finished paintings and decided that between us we
had the makings of a respectable exhibition. If we were
to be serious artists we must begin to show our work in

public and start to build our reputations. We eyed the walls of the Royal Conservatory of Music and took courage in hand.

"An interview with Dr. MacMillan [not yet Sir Ernest], most gracious of men, made us feel instantly at ease as he chatted away about our sketches as if he had nothing on earth to do but entertain us."

We framed up and hung about twenty small oils in the lunchroom and corridors of the conservatory. No sales, of course, although at ten dollars framed the prices were moderate, but we had the satisfaction of seeing the work properly presented and feeling that it looked professional.

We were working and playing hard. My diary is full of parties in Curry's room, of serious discussions about art and life, about the possibility of getting a job at the new technical school that was due to open in north Toronto in the next year. But in the meantime the family was anticipating big doings at Christmas. Ken and Betty were coming home from Toledo with their baby, and Doug and Audrey were to be married at our house on New Year's Eve.

Christmas was like all family Christmases with new babies: exciting, hectic, and emotional. And the wedding preparations were even more so. Audrey's mother was dead, and she had no real home. She had been living as a companion to a woman whose husband had begun to make passes at her, and her father and brother were sharing a single room and could offer no solution. Mother invited her to stay with us until the end of the year. But Mother and Audrey were temperamentally incompatible, and as Audrey became more tense and uncomfortable, Mother became more critical and irritated. I began to wonder if they could last until the wedding without an explosion.

New Year's Eve brought an ice storm that made Balsam Avenue hill impassable. The minister who was to perform the ceremony was three-quarters of an hour late and arrived eventually on foot, without his wife. Doug and Audrey were to go up to Kapuskasing by train that night so that Doug could resume his job on January 2. Doug's best man began to drive them to the station, but his car developed a flat tire a few blocks from home, the nearby taxi company just laughed at Doug's request for a car on a New Year's Eve in that weather, and the poor bride and groom had to pile in on top of their friends in the pursuing car and be driven ingloriously to the station. Doug boasts that they had the last laugh, because their tickets let them through the barrier and into the Pullman, where they were able to lock themselves away before the rest of us could buy platform tickets.

I fled to Haliburton the next day, joining Curry and Ruth and Casey, two others of our college gang, who had been painting for a week already.

"January 7, 1930: This is really the period of New Year's reflections and resolves, for Jan. 1 was a whirl of busyness this year. But even now I feel not in the least retrospective. Gone, and it was a good year, that's all. Come, and it promises well. Lindsay accomplished its usual magic this morning. Once there, my regrets at leaving Haliburton gave place to joy at the thoughts of greeting Toronto once more. Returning to school filled me with shivers of delight. Kay and I met, and kissed, and rejoiced in each other, and there were Archie and Fran, and Leslie and Tong, and Ed leaping at me, and there

were Curry and Casey, just as natural as I had left them
in the morning, and suddenly I found myself truly back
at school, perhaps for the last time in just this way. Both
Dad and Mother like my sketches, which pleases me.
They *are* better. I feel it myself."

"Monday, February 3: Life is moving around me very
quickly. Two things happened today that seem to be
hustling me out of the irresponsibility and freedom of my
life so far, and into the workaday world of grown up.
Mother made an appointment for me with Mr. Saunders,
my future principal if there should be a post for me at
Northern Vocational School, and Arthur Lismer offered
me a Saturday-morning teaching job. I don't want to be
teaching so soon! I cling to my last happy independent
year – but truly such is life." By this time I had accepted
teaching as the most practical way for me to be an artist.
I recognized that being an artist had to be first with me,
at least until I was swept off my feet by the Right Man
and offered another kind of life.

After two years of painting, free-lance lecturing, and
teaching, Arthur Lismer had been taken on by the Toronto Art Gallery as director of education, with a Carne-
gie grant to enable him to introduce a new concept in art
education for children. It was now thought that the
purpose of teaching art should be to release and encour-
age a child's own creativity, rather than to develop technical skills. Professor Cizek of Czechoslovakia had
brought a wonderful exhibition of children's paintings to
the Toronto Art Gallery that had illustrated the value of
this approach. Lismer was inspired by the possibilities,

and he inspired everyone who worked with him. We made a modest start that first year, but by the next fall we had hundreds of children, picked by their public-school teachers as the most talented and interested, and further screened by us at the gallery. Curry was taken on the staff, along with three or four others, and Curry and I were the team responsible for all the eleven-year-olds, boys and girls. We had sixty of them between us. Eleven is the perfect age. At eleven children have lost none of their openness and energy and have not yet become self-critical or inhibited.

Because Curry and I had the largest group, we were usually put to work in the Long Gallery, which was just beyond the sculpture court. Before the Toronto Art Gallery became the Art Gallery of Ontario, it had already known one major expansion from the original Grange House, home of the Baldwins, by the addition on its north side of a big building containing a square sculpture court, flanked on three sides by rectangular galleries in which we held the Saturday-morning activities. Offices and the library were still in the old Grange House, which had not yet been restored to its nineteenth-century beauty. Grange House was where we would have a get-together with Lismer and the other teachers, perhaps over coffee, to plan a theme for the next week or to contrive some new medium to excite the kids.

When the next week came we were on our own, organizing the materials, presenting the challenge, and ducking out of the way to avoid the stampede as our eleven-year-olds rushed to get started. They spread their work on the floor and knelt over it. We provided big brushes, generous pots of colour, as much paper as they could use. We encouraged, praised, suggested further development, but made no attempt to impose our ideas on them. They were bursting with ideas of their own. This was the essence of Lismer's new concept, and a revolutionary change from what I had known as art in public school, where we had been set with hard pencils to copy strawberry boxes or paint sprays of red salvia in September with miserable thin camel's-hair brushes and dry cakes of water-colour.

From our children we wanted personal involvement and imagination, not copying. We told them fairy stories to give them ideas, took them along Dundas Street to watch the Eaton's Santa Claus parade, asked them to illustrate a house fire or moving day, and let them make masks or fantastic costumes of brown paper and newsprint, cut up and painted. At the end of the morning we gathered an armful of startlingly original drawings and paintings, collected the left-over materials, and carried everything back to Grange House for storage, and to show to Lismer and the other teachers. There we would find Lismer already off on a new tack, three jumps ahead of us.

After the turn of the year all the students in fourth year at the college were working under pressure, with exams looming and projects to be finished. But at the end of March, Marjorie and I achieved a weekend together. We went out to the Falcon Inn at West Hill, a charming English-style hotel that burned down a few years later. Mother was critical of the idea, having heard dark reports of the goings-on there: drinking, businessmen and their secretaries in illicit liaisons, and who knows what else. In the event, we were the only guests that weekend, and as

the silence descended at about eight-thirty, when the
kitchen closed up for the night, we were hard put to
suppress our giggles. We walked, we read, we talked, and
came back with our feathers smoothed into place, and a
great thankfulness that we were going to be together at
Camp Tanamakoon for the whole summer coming. This
was the Margaret Eaton camp in Algonquin Park that
Marjorie had enjoyed so much the previous year.

I returned with renewed zest to school. Drawing and
painting from the nude model, life-size, in oil on canvas,
was the major work of senior painting students, occupy-
ing every morning. I had long since learned to stretch and
prepare my own canvases on wooden frames and man-
handle them back and forth from school on the streetcar.
Afternoons were given to still life painting, again in oil on
large canvases. In second and third years we had worked
briefly in water-colour from a clothed model, but water-
colour was a neglected medium at the college, perhaps
reflecting its general fall from fashion. Lettering and
design were dropped in fourth year unless a student had
chosen the commercial art option. Everyone took history
of art and anatomy, both after-hours lecture courses
demanding written exams. Other examinations were
practical tests in which we had several days to carry a
project through to completion under supervision. Because I was very interested in sculpture I had obtained
permission to take night classes with Emanuel Hahn and
carry a double specialization, painting and sculpture,
with my sculpture examination scheduled for every evening during one week in May. For that week I arranged
to stay uptown with Curry. I observed that on May 7 the
chestnut trees, which in those days lined St. George

Street, were in tender curly leaf. Every year since, I have checked the trees on that date to see if we are ahead or behind 1930.

The end of term came too soon. "Friday, May 9: An idyllic day, with sunlight that made the world look unreal and lovely, and a mad gambol at recess among the dandelions, a beautiful noon hour prone in green grass, yellow golden flowers and flower-like children, a jolly dinner, and a gay feeling of nonsense. Casey, ungraciously enough, asked me to the dance, but at least I am going. Praise be."

Our graduation dinner was to be held at the Arts and Letters Club, with the class going on to dance at the Royal York Hotel. The Arts and Letters Club was a beautiful place, formerly a church, high-ceilinged Gothic, in dark wood, hung with heraldic banners, romantic, and full of association with the great men of our world of art. The most famous historic photograph of the Group of Seven was taken there at lunch the day they adopted their name. For tonight's special occasion, the head table ran the length of the room, with its line-up of special guests and staff. J.E.H. MacDonald, now the principal, was in the centre, and ranged out from him were Beatty, Franz Johnston, Mr. Hahn, Herbie Stansfield, and the junior teachers. The rest of us were at small tables in front of them. Of the sixty students who had been in first year together only seven were graduating, and each of us was given a yellow rose to wear to distinguish us from the other students and guests. We seven were all dressed up and keyed up.

One of the first features of the evening after dinner was the farewell speech by Robert Holmes, a dear old boy who had taught us history of art, a painter notable for his very fine water-colours of Canadian wild flowers, who was due for retirement. He opened his speech with an affectionate tribute to the school itself, and was just starting to talk about the students, when he hesitated, stopped, and suddenly fell behind the table.

"The dinner began so beautifully and before we had realized what had happened Death was there. We were helpless – we stood in horror-stricken groups without speaking, and heard the rattle in his throat, and saw his face go grey and then opaque, and people doing things, Ed and Mac chafing his hands, Bernard fanning him, Mac listening for his heart. Mr. Beatty, who had been reviling Mr. Reid a minute before, trying to detect a cloud on a magnifying glass. Miss Coombs, here and there as she was needed, face set. Mr. Johnston, self-possessed, telling us how fitting it was, the unreality of it all, people with rouge over pale faces, eyes to the ground, smelling their yellow roses, Curry's hand in mine, the terrible wait for a doctor, the damp, fresh night, the weight of horror clouding future memories, the petty regrets about parties and graduation."

We drifted home to Curry's room and sat on the floor in front of her fire, needing one another for comfort. To avoid the long trip home after the dance at the Royal York, I had arranged to stay with Curry, and when the others had gone, we went to bed, but we slept badly.

When I went into the college in the morning to clear my locker, there was a phone call for me. It was Mother. Dad had had a hemorrhage during the night and was in St. Michael's Hospital. Would I please come directly there?

"And then this morning Mother's phone call – and Mr. Holmes's face leapt to my mind, and I fought tears and knew it was nerves and yet was sick with terror and dread. I tried to tell Curry, but there were others there, so all I could do was hang onto her hard and cry on her shoulder. Ed was so great, drove me down to the hospital with Curry, and waited. When I had seen Dad I felt quite released because he looked pale but normal, and talked to me and was just Dad."

9

Grim Reality

TANAMAKOON did not give me the summer with Marjorie
that I had imagined. True, we were both there, but not
together. She was part of the group of beautiful, assured
senior counsellors, all old friends from last year. I was a
new assistant craft teacher, doing what I was told, directed by a woman who knew her basketwork and
leathercraft but was no artist. I was responsible for half
a dozen fourteen-year-olds, with whom I sat at table, and
whose cabin life I shared and supervised. I found it hard
to relate to them. At our first meal together they were
discussing the pros and cons of the various ships on which
they had crossed the Atlantic. They came from a world
that was unknown to me, and I resented their criticism of
the excellent food and their complaints about what
seemed to me luxurious living in the camp.

"July 4, 1930: I still have a queer feeling that it's a
purposeless sort of place, and I wonder what on earth is

the soul of camp for them. For so long camp to me has been fellowship, intensely, with God and my friends, and the joy of little intimate customs and occasions. Here my cabin assure me that they never talk about religion. Marjorie is hither and yon, and I'm busy with duties and confabs, and life is very full without visiting her, but I'm wondering if she'll come to say good night. Only three days of my teens left."

"July 5: With a horrible inferiority complex and a feeling of most complete uselessness – in the way if I'm with my cabin and guilty if I'm enjoying life alone or with any other counsellors. Haven't seen M today, except across the dining room. This is not what I call camp!"

The news from home was disturbing. Dad's illness had been diagnosed as stomach ulcer, and I had left for the summer confident that he was on the mend. But Mother wrote that "spinach and motoring are off Dad's list," and that alarmed me. Why should he not be *adding* foods and activities?

Camp improved with the weeks as the campers and I began to appreciate it more. I still felt excluded from the inner circle of old counsellors who surrounded Marjorie, but I found kindred souls on the fringe. We had precious half-days when two counsellors were free to leave the camp after lunch and to be out until after breakfast the next morning. That meant a chance to take a canoe across several portages into Canoe Lake, visit the famous Taylor Statten camps there – Wapomea for girls and Ahmek for boys – where Gordon Webber was art counsellor, and sleep on the home side of the last portage, within reach of the deadline. Gordon was a friend from public school,

where he had been notable for receiving more valentines
than anyone else in the class. He had lived on Maclean
Avenue and been part of that gang. He was one of the
College of Art students who had pulled out and gone with
the Art Students' League when Mr. Lismer left. And
recently he had come with his family to live in the big
house to the north of us, and to drop in often for a gossip
about our common world of art. We were friends on many
different levels. Gordon had had one withered leg since
infancy and was always dramatically lame. Recently the
leg had been amputated, and Gordon's casual attitude
towards "Darby," the artificial substitute, was one of his
many engaging characteristics.

On one of the free half-days, Margot Gordon, the
Tanamakoon drama counsellor, and I picked him up at
Camp Ahmek and carried him off for a shore supper on
one of the islands on Canoe Lake. We talked late around
our little fire, and when we came to paddle him back to
his camp, a heavy evening mist had blotted out the edges
of the lake. It was utterly still. We dropped our voices to
listen to the silence, and as we felt our way through the
mist, Gordon told us in hushed tones the story that was
gaining credence in the park, the rumour that Tom Thom-
son, whose cairn on the hill we had passed that afternoon,
had actually been murdered.

We let Gordon out at the dock, and he vanished into
the night. We turned away and crept along close to the
edge of the lake, swerving to avoid the deadheads that
loomed at us out of the fog, poking into every little bay to
look for the beginning of the portage. We were very quiet.
It was an eerie trip, each portage hard to find, increas-

ingly difficult to cross as we struggled under the growing weight of the canoe and our packs. The last and longest portage was broken by Koochie Pond.

"Never shall I forget the exhaustion of that dreadful portage. I felt that I couldn't bear it for another step – but we stumbled on to Koochie, and there I lay, numb with weariness and the hopelessness of ever being able to move. I would try to sit up, and fall again onto our bedding rolls, knowing that Koochie was too marshy for a camping spot, but without the strength to struggle on. Margot, fortunately, was a little less done out, so we crossed the pond and were pulling the canoe out on the other side when we missed our pack. Margot jumped in again and pushed out, and for a bad fifteen minutes we were separated, cut off completely by darkness and too sensitive to the stillness and mystery of the place to call to each other. I sat drunkenly on the moss and tried to read the sounds, the knock of her paddle on the gunwale, the occasional drip or splash – a long pause – again a knock – then a huge splash and silence. Had she fallen in? I hadn't the strength to rescue her. 'Margot, are you all right?' No answer, but at last the knock, knock again, and the canoe sliding towards me out of the darkness. 'It was a beaver,' said Margot. 'It scared me too.'"

We left the canoe where it was. Margot carried the bedding, while I carried the little flashlight, my arm aching from shoulder to wrist with its weight. Morning came early, and we woke to see with interest the world we had camped in. Partridgeberry around us, a few 'ghost flowers,' and the welcome sun, fears admitted and laughed at. And while Margot rolled the pack, I trotted across to Koochie and almost danced back with the canoe. Gone the misgivings – gone the weariness – gone the ache from my shoulders! On the far shore of White Lake we could see the roofs of Tanamakoon, home safe!

"August 26: Mother says Dad is getting weaker and losing heart, a cold terror to hear. I can't bear to think of it. I won't believe it till I must. Poor Mother. This summer must have been hell for her." Hell indeed. Mother had known before I went north that it was cancer, but she decided to let me have the summer free of that burden. And Dad was not to be told. Mother wanted to leave him hope.

We still had to live through the fall, watching him become paler and more frail. There was the day he taught me to change the washer on a tap, and my throat ached with the effort to keep back the tears and give no sign that I knew why I had to learn to do it. Later there was the day that Mother had to bring home the papers from the safety deposit box and have them all explained to her. And no words. Mother and I talked to each other but neither of us talked with Dad. I wouldn't have known what words to use, even if I had been allowed to speak. My diary is so tear-spotted that much of it is illegible. But at least I could write my grief.

Every day Mother helped Dad to dress, and he sat downstairs, not even reading, but rousing when someone called, and many did. The September night that Laurie Bullen and Dorothy Dodd, his old date from the Malvern days, were married, Mother and I went to the church, remembering how we had all been together for Doug's wedding less than a year ago. In Malvern days Laurie had been like another son around our place, and the boys had gone together into engineering. Later that night Laurie's

mother came to the house, still in her gold lamé finery,
bringing Dad the bride's bouquet, with Dorothy's special
love. Dr. Cotton dropped by often, casually, as a neighbour and a friend. Everyone was doggedly cheerful. I
have often wondered if Dad would have liked to talk with
us about what we were all facing.

Mother had moved Dad into the big north bedroom
with the sunroom off it. A day came in November when
she couldn't rouse him, and his breathing was harsh.
Mother called Mrs. Trowell, Grandmother's cousin, and
she came down for moral support. I had taken over the
small back bedroom as a studio, and I was slugging away
at the Christmas cards that were my best hope of income
that fall. About noon, Mrs. Trowell called Mother down
to have some lunch, and I took over the vigil. While I sat
with my hand covering one of his, he stopped breathing.
That was all.

"Saturday, November 15: For ages I wondered if I'd
ever feel like writing again and doubted it, but perhaps it
was having Dad's pen made me want to, to taste the joy
of having it and to remember from years past the respect
and almost awe that I held Dad's pen in, his care of it, and
his care and method in keeping everything he valued.
He's left us a heritage of dependability if only we are able
to accept it."

Dad was still in his fifties when he died, still an active
city engineer until that dreadful night of my graduation
when he was first taken ill. I felt a kind of bitter recognition that he had completed his most important responsibilities, seen his three children educated, and made sure
that Mother had her home paid for and enough income
to live on before he was free to die.

"I'm glad I went to the cemetery. M was with me, and I watched the trees, bare-branched against the pale sky, and wondered about the flowers. I told myself that it really wasn't Dad – and it didn't matter. Mother talks about how happy he must be with his old friends, and I can't feel anything except a fierce pride in him and in our love for each other, and a fierce resentment that my children won't know him or care. I can't bear to think that in another generation he will be unknown, that the City Hall people perhaps don't really care, even now, that his whole fine life will be forgotten even while the things he did are going on, and I loved him so. One of my biggest comforts is that I didn't have to wait for him to go to discover how much I loved him, and that for some reason the tears stayed back and I could be calm."

Mother retreated into black widowhood, with a heavy crape veil falling from her hat. It had some point. People knew enough not to ask her about her husband, and everyone was kind and considerate in shops and on the streetcar. After her long, faithful ordeal of nursing him, I didn't begrudge her the drama.

My concern now was to start to earn a living. We were a year into the Great Depression. Commercial art firms were laying off staff. I had seen Fred Brigden's paintings many times and even met him, so I took my portfolio to Brigden's, the advertising agency I knew to have been the nursery of many of Canada's artists. Mr. Brigden told me that I might work for them to gain experience if I wanted, but they could not pay me. My concern was to be able to give Mother money for my board and I decided to go on

free-lancing. The Saturday-morning classes at the art
gallery provided a steady income of five dollars a week.
Moulton College, a private school for girls, gave me two
half-days teaching a week. Leadership of a CGIT group at
one of the inner-city churches meant a small honorarium.
In the back of my diary I kept track of all my free-lance
work and what it brought in. That first year I made
twenty-seven posters for various people and occasions,
for as little as fifty cents each and as much as four dollars.
I wrote and illuminated the oath of allegiance for the
Ontario Boys' Parliament (fourteen dollars), and I continued to do black-and-white drawings for the United
Church and CGIT. My biggest item was Christmas cards.
I made and peddled hundreds of dozens of lino blocks of
Haliburton winter scenes, printing and colouring them
by hand in up to eight colours and making the envelopes
to match.

In a different category in my mind were sales of paintings, six oil sketches that first year, usually for ten dollars
each, which must have included frames. When Louise
Boothe, the Beaches librarian and Marjorie's CGIT leader,
bought three I cut the price for her. Another oil sketch
was sold to the Beaches Library Drama League, perhaps
as a cast gift to a director. A Malvern friend, now a
graduate of U of T, chose a Haliburton winter scene, and
a leader at one of my CGIT county camps wanted one I
had painted at Beau Rivage, the leadership camp on the
St. Lawrence. At that time ten dollars a week seemed a
fair price for board, and I discovered later that Mother
banked the lot in a special account that she kept in trust
for me. With the balance of what I earned I was able to
clothe myself, pay for streetcar tickets, and buy my art

supplies, as well as save a bit, as I was always a firm believer in Mr. Micawber's recipe for happiness.

Early in the new year Mother went into hospital for an operation that the doctors hoped would cure the misery she had been living with for too long, a painful condition of the tissues of the rectum. "February 12, 1931: Mother phoned just a little while ago to say that she was having another operation this afternoon, instead of coming home as she had hoped. Poor Mum. The house is spotless. I cleaned it from top to bottom yesterday, and today I feel very let down to think that it must be done over again in a few days."

"February 24: Mother wanted to know tonight if I were using Dutch Cleanser on my teeth! What next?"

While Mother was in hospital, high up in the Private Patients' Pavilion of the Toronto General Hospital, I painted a canvas of the view from her window, looking south to the dramatic height – for 1931 – of the new Royal York Hotel, which was seen dominating the skyline. In the foreground were the workmen's cottages that crowded the district, known then as "the Ward." I submitted it to the Ontario Society of Artists' annual open exhibition and it was accepted. My excitement at this success was tempered by disappointment that Curry's work was rejected.

"March 5, 1931: After the first little kick, my pleasure is lost because Curry didn't have one hung, and hers are so much better and for many reasons I wish it had been she. Poor kid – she's had so much to discourage her that I do wish she'd been lucky this time."

"March 7: Yesterday was immense! A telegram first thing to announce Doug's baby – and the thought of them, with a little red baby – and them so thrilled with it, just made the day! And then we were too excited to be coherent in a telegram, and finally sent one each in our enthusiasm. The OSA opening at night was queer. I'm ashamed of my canvas, and many things made me rather miserable, but it was fun in its way, and a start."

"March 11: A letter from Jessie from the north today, out of the blue, saying 'congratulations.' Congratulations are the funniest things to me – I can't even realize what they're for. Today, reading Joseph Conrad's words about art, I recognized for the first time that my poor little canvas was, while I was working on it, genuinely sincere. Perhaps more thought and labour went into it than usual, and I really did have an idea to express. But I expressed it so inadequately!"

Juried shows were an opportunity for young artists to view their work in the company of paintings by the top professionals. The societies held such shows annually, electing each year a different committee of their most experienced and respected members to act as a jury. Anyone could submit work if it was framed ready for exhibition and the modest entry fee was paid. Sometimes there were prizes offered for "best in the show" or for the best in some special category. Admission to membership in the societies had to be earned by having one's work regularly accepted for hanging, and at that time the rule in the Ontario Society of Artists was that only candidates who had been successful in the three previous years could be considered for membership. One year missed meant starting all over again.

I had now put my foot on the first rung of the ladder, but it was to be a few more years before I could go to an opening of a juried show and see my work among all the others with any satisfaction. I was overjoyed to be accepted, and sick with disappointment when the mail brought a rejection slip, but a juried show is a stern test. In a solo show the sum of the exhibition speaks more eloquently than any single work. In a juried show there is a babel of voices, all talking at once, the paintings often so close together that they compete for attention and the one with the most strident voice is the one that is apt to be noticed. Juried shows were good proving grounds where I could assess the strengths and weaknesses of my work in challenging company.

10

Miss McCarthy, Teacher

NORAH MCCULLOUGH, who was Lismer's full-time assistant at the art gallery, alerted me late in 1931 that her friend Edith Manning, a teacher in the art department of Central Technical School, was to be married at Christmas. In those days, marriage meant dismissal for a woman teacher. Her job would be open. I had already tried to be taken on staff at the new Northern Vocational School, but I had been turned down as too young at twenty. But I was now twenty-one, and Charles Goldhamer was at Central; he had taught me at the college and had been very friendly and interested in my progress whenever our paths had crossed since. I telephoned him to ask how I should go about applying, and he set up an appointment for me with the art director, Peter Haworth.

Central Tech, opened in 1914, was the first technical school in Toronto, and the last school to be built in the euphoria before the Great War. It was a handsome grey stone building with an imposing Gothic entrance approached by a wide flight of steps, surmounted by a square stone tower. For my night classes in swimming I had entered at a corner door and gone right downstairs to the changing rooms and the pool. The approach up the stairs to the front door was much more impressive, and I was directed from there up two more wide flights to Mr. Haworth's office at the head of the stairs on the third floor.

Mr. Haworth gave an occasional grunt as he looked over the portfolio I had brought and asked me some questions, especially about the outdoor painting I had done, but he didn't commit himself to anything. He did ask me if I thought I could teach a group of librarians how to make posters, and when I assured him that I could, he told me to be at the school before nine o'clock on January 4, the first day after the Christmas holidays, prepared to do just that.

I was there as directed, standing in the front hall waiting for him, trying not to look as awkward as I felt. He showed me where to sign the register for pay purposes, and as we were on our way over to the big flight of stairs up to the art department, he stopped me in front of an imposing-looking man, ruddy of face, ruddy of hair, standing like a statue in the hall.

"You'd better meet the man who runs this place."

"Dr. Kirkland?" I asked, offering my hand. Peter kept his face straight with some difficulty, and explained to me later as we climbed the steps that the heroic figure was Major Simpson-Ray, the chief caretaker, and not the principal, as I had assumed.

At that time, Peter Haworth was a young, good-looking, curly-headed autocrat, who was gradually trans-

forming a mediocre secondary school art department into
a dynamic powerhouse. He was given unusual freedom
in choosing his staff, and instead of hiring teachers who
had taken summer courses in art, he hired artists and
hoped that they could teach. He encouraged them to go
on being artists and fought a stand-up battle at the Board
of Education on the issue. Someone down at College
Street (where the central authority for the Toronto Board
of Education was located) attempted to forbid him to
practise as a stained-glass designer while he was holding
down a full-time teaching job. This was during the Depression, and the stained-glass trade was feeling the competition. But he won, not just for himself but for all the
artists and craftsmen in the system. He convinced the
authorities that an effective teacher must also be a practising artist.

Peter's method of teacher training was to fling his
novices into the situation and let them fight their own way
to the surface. He explained nothing, and his manner
discouraged questions. When I reported to his office, as
instructed, after my class with the librarians, he said to
me only, "You can take PG1GH in EM3 this afternoon."

I found someone, I have forgotten whom, to translate.
PG1GH meant Pre-vocational Girls, first year, sections G
and H. EM3 turned out to be the classroom up in the tower.
How could I ever have guessed that? Every day I reported to Mr. Haworth's office and received my instructions in code. I was told where to get a supply of drawing
paper, and little else.

"Tuesday: In a state of headache, weariness, worry,
and hoarseness, I think I won't be a teacher after all. I
don't honestly see any fun in trying to get twenty bored

twelve-year-olds to draw a silly coal scuttle that they can't draw anyhow. Damn them. I wish I were home cursing the rolling hills of Haliburton for not rolling themselves into a good composition for me, and my head aches." For that first nightmare week, I lived from minute to minute, with no timetable in advance and no briefing on what I was expected to teach. "I feel that I should be recording first impressions but they are still too hectic to be very easily expressed. I'm dead sick of waiting around to see Mr. Haworth, and still lost when I wander away from the art department, and I wish heartily that I had a locker to call my own, and every hour I get dizzier and dizzier like Saturday mornings, in spite of which I begin to feel a little exhilaration at having a job and enjoy telling people. If only my head would stop aching, and my cold would clear up, I think I could recover my mental balance."

Once the first week was over, and I had not been fired, I began to realize that I had inherited Edith Manning's timetable as well as her job. My classes were not art students. In most cases they were "vocationals" or, worse still, "pre-vocationals," youngsters unable to make it in the academic stream who were given watered-down courses in English and mathematics and allowed to concentrate on cooking and sewing, with physical training and art to round out the week. They were toughies, ready to walk all over an inexperienced teacher. These kids were regarded as the bottom of the totem pole, but I also was at the bottom of the totem pole, and grateful to have a place on it at all.

It was also true that nobody in the art department cared about them, and I was free to do anything with them that would keep them out of trouble. If, by using all my native wit and my CGIT experience, I could find projects they liked, and show them how to produce presentable work, we were even allowed a small stretch of wall to exhibit the results. This was how I discovered the magic of cut paper as a medium, easier than drawing, faster than painting, spectacular, and fun. With sheets of coloured paper, chosen for colour harmony and tone contrast, they could hardly go wrong.

One afternoon when I was teaching, not in the art department up on the fourth floor, but down on B floor in an academic classroom, I was startled by a roar from a stout man standing in the open doorway. "Who is in charge of this class?" "I am," meekly. "Who are you?" And I found myself at last meeting my principal, Dr. Kirkland. It was a poor start, but the only bad moment I ever had with him.

It was in the spring of 1932 that Grandfather Moffatt lost his job, almost without warning. He had been with the income tax department in Montreal. He felt that they showed very little appreciation of his years of faithful work and the tremendous sums he had tracked down in tax evasions when they turned him out on his eightieth birthday. Grandmother was not well, and, after some soul-searching, Mother invited them to come to Toronto and live with us. There was room. Mother gave them the big front bedroom and the small room beside it that had been mine. She moved into the north room where Dad had been at the last. I made the upstairs sitting room into my bedroom but kept my little studio at the back.

If it was hard for us to do all this reorganization, for

them the uprooting must have been shattering. Grandma had kept house and bossed Grandpa for more than fifty years, and now she was doomed to live in another woman's home. Some of her treasures came with her, but most of her furniture had to be left behind. She was unhappy, and so was Mother. Grandpa did everything he could to keep them simmered down, but he had his own problems. He wanted, naturally enough, to be the man in the house for Mother's sake, and to relieve her of furnace duty. But Mother had been taught how to run the furnace by Dad. It was a coal burner, stoked by Dad every morning and left alone until he came back after work. According to Mother, that was the only way to run the furnace. But Grandfather, who had nothing to do all day long except nurse the fire, knew that the most economical way was to add a bit of coal every hour, and keep it always burning steadily. I laugh about it now, but at the time it was not funny to Mother. She took it as a criticism of Dad, who, now that he was gone, could do no wrong.

Grandpa had a saving sense of humour and a gentle irony, which I enjoyed, but which neither of his other women shared. Grandmother's face would tighten, and she would look at him in reproof. "Archie!"

At school, I was beginning to enjoy the other young artists on the staff. Closest to me was Noreen Masters, tall, dark, vivid, a magnet for anything male, and a scandal to some of the older academic teachers. Nory had a sense of style and designed her own clothes. The form-fitting silver satin gown that she appeared in at the Teachers' Federation dance caused a sensation. Irene Doole, who was a perfect lady, approached me in the staff room the next day. Had I been at the ball? Well, no, actually I

hadn't. I had, however, seen the dress and Nory in it.
Irene intimated that she was speaking to me because she
believed me to be a friend, and what Noreen needed was
"a friend to tell her." I'm afraid I told her all right,
gleefully.

Nory had been a student in the Central Tech art
department, a young artist of such brilliance that she had
been invited back the year after her graduation to take
over the classes in illustration. She had imagination and
could stimulate it in her students. Before the annual
bazaar she had her classes working on posters eight feet
high. Her own walls were filled, and every other room in
the department had three or four of these huge posters
covering the back wall. The students worked where they
could find space. Art staff drifted in and out of all the
rooms, approving, criticizing. We got used to the chaos
and found the excitement contagious.

Mr. Haworth asked me to make one of these posters
to advertise the work of the Vocationals, a grim task for
me, feeling as I did that it would be in competition with
the best work of the senior students. However, remembering what even the Pre-vocationals had produced, I
used cut paper, hid my insecurity, and got away with it.

The annual exhibition in March was a time of reckoning
when you could see the quality of the years' work. The
week after it, Mr. Haworth called me in to the office. Did
I want to go on teaching? The truthful answer would have
been no, but even in that first difficult term there had been
moments of exhilaration, and I needed the job, so my
answer was yes. If I were to go on, Mr. Haworth explained, I would be wise to qualify by taking the teacher
training course and getting a certificate. Then I could be

taken on staff and paid an annual salary instead of wages by the half-day. Some points were stretched to convince the Ontario Training College for Technical Teachers that I had the equivalent of six years' experience in the trade, and, since my academic qualifications were high, I was somewhat grudgingly granted permission to enter the school in Hamilton the following September.

All during the winter I was painting hard, developing some of my Haliburton sketches into canvases. The previous year Curry and Casey and I had hung a joint exhibition of sketches at Annesley Hall, the women's residence of Victoria College. This year I sent a solo show to Strathcona Hall of McGill University in Montreal. Later I was part of a group show in the Memorial Hall of St. Aidan's church. "Monday, February 29, 1932: This has been an interesting weekend. Thursday night the exhibit down at St Aidan's opened, and people said so many nice things about my Snow Drift canvas that a perfect fever of excitement and ambition and dreaming laid hold on me, and I was thrilled and yet embarrassed by every compliment. I think they are very bad for me but I have a great appetite for appreciation."

I submitted two canvases for the OSA annual juried show and lived in suspense. "Wednesday, March 2: I telephoned today to ask about my canvases and Mother had no news and sounded very disappointed, so I went back up the stairs to the life room feeling very flat, and I sat on the edge of the table and went into a daze, while the bad little prevocationals chattered. I wanted so much for one of my things to be hung! I almost called home to ask about the afternoon mail but decided that that would be too eager. Mother was out mailing a letter when I

turned the corner of Pine and she had the news for me.
One accepted! I expect it is the Frozen Lake. Wish now
I had sent the Drift too, except that I know perfectly well
if I had sent the Drift, I should be regretting not having
tried one of the others."

"Friday, March 4: Tonight has really been rather wonderful, my beloved black velvet making me feel beautiful
(comparatively) and slim and well-groomed, with the
white rabbit's-fur wrap to add soft luxury and M's yellow
roses to say that she was loving me on my Big Night. It
was fun being with Mother because I could run off when
I felt like it and have my little side chat with Nancy
Caudle [fellow artist from Malvern days] and Gilbert
Schlater [of OCA] and so forth. The 'Moulton Line' [from
Moulton College] was strung along in front of my picture,
being very rapturous when I first found it. It was all a bit
sweet and silly, absolutely different from last year." The
big difference was that this time I was not ashamed of the
canvas.

1932 was the spring of my first car. Curry's brother,
Ronald, was ready to sell his little Chev convertible, blue,
with a rumble seat at the back. I saw it when I was in
Haliburton at Easter, painting with Curry. Once the
roads were open again after the spring break-up, Ron
drove it down to Toronto, picked me up at the Beach, and
took me out to the Exhibition grounds for my first and
only driving lesson. What a marvellous feeling! I was
surprised, and disappointed, that he wouldn't let me keep
the wheel for the drive home through the city.

The Shawnees were ecstatic about the car, which they

christened Gabriel. It gave us mobility and made our weekend camps easier of access. It also made possible the mural painting I had been given permission to do on the walls of the children's room at the Earlscourt Library.

George Reid, now retired as principal of the College of Art, had done a mural around the walls of the adult room of this library. Louise Boothe suggested that I might like to try my hand at a mural, and the very thought was thrilling to me, intimidating but alluring. I went up to see the Reid mural and measure the walls of the children's room so that I could prepare a sketch to scale for Louise to show to the Library Board. The board, having approved my sketch, agreed to pay for the paint that I would use. All that wonderful experience at no expense to me!

"March 23: Today I trekked out to Mr. Reid's for a very nice visit, and the delight of tea in his beautiful home, pewter things on the mantel, dusty rich coloured hangings over the balcony, lovely mellowed wooden chairs, a glorious room! And he was a very gracious host besides being helpful about the mural. I feel quite as if I *were* going to decorate the library. It seems just a question of getting the ladder and starting in."

I used fairy tales as my motifs, and the space was generous enough to allow the figures to be life-size, with the giant of Jack and the Beanstalk twice that. The paintings filled all four sides above the bookcases. The walls were coarse-textured plaster, agreeable to paint on, and I didn't mind the height and all the climbing up and down on the scaffolding. The caretaker considered the weeks I put in on the job excessive since he had seen a man paint a whole billboard in a single day, but he was my only critic. When the work was finished, the board gave me an exhibition in the adult room, a party at the opening, and, best of all, a surprise cheque for two hundred dollars.

There were some congenial young teachers at Central Tech who drifted toward the lunch table where the art department usually gathered. Amos Culligan – Mully – as Irish as his name, was a mathematician who had developed a course that art students could relate to and relish. Mully would argue about anything, outrageously but with humour.

Jimmy Dean, the young head of the mathematics department, was an enthusiastic promoter of drama at the school and he decided that spring to stage an all-staff production. He put on *Mr. Pim Passes By*, with Nory and himself playing the juvenile leads, and me the lovely fat part of Olivia. Rehearsing with teachers from other departments of the school was a good way to make friends with them, and we played to a full auditorium for two or three nights.

"May 15: It's Sunday. Last night was the final night of Mr. Pim – a mixture of delight and horror. George and I got beautifully twisted in our second act, in a quite original way, and went doggedly along picking up prompts gratefully. But at least everything went well, and nobody was any the wiser. Curry said afterwards that she was thrilled, and amazingly enough Mother liked it."

After that I began to feel at home with the other teachers on the staff, and in the halls I was less apt to be mistaken for a student.

Dad as a young man, 1922.

Mother at the age of eighteen, photographed in the gown she wore as a professional soprano soloist.

Grandfather and Grandmother Moffatt, photographed in the dining room at Balsam Avenue, 1926.

Doug, Kenneth, and Doris, 1922.

Our beloved Florrie, 1915.

On the dock at Silver Island,
1922: Marjorie and Doris in
made-to-order play-suits and
Mother with groceries from
the supply boat.

Debut of a playwright at the St. Aidan's
church concert, 1921: "This day is an
epoch in my life."

The Shawnees en route to their first camp at Orr Lake, 1930.

Marjorie at Normandale, 1927; on the hill behind, the dining pavilion known as the "shack."

Mary Allison and Jessie Macpherson at the CGIT provincial leadership camp, Beausoleil Island, 1927.

An OCA sketching party at Riverbend Lodge, Kitchener, 1927.
Arthur Lismer, top left; Doris McCarthy, far right.

J.W. Beatty and group at the Port Hope Summer School, 1929.
Beatty, top left; bottom left: Margaret Stevenson, Frances Anne
Johnston in the striped toque, Narcisse Pelletier in the dark beret,
Ruth Dingle, and Franklin Arbuckle with a newspaper.

The summer at North Lake, 1932. Two views of Curry, at work and posed at the door of the hunting cabin, and Doris with canvases and paint box, paddling back to camp.

Doris and Curry with the Chev and trailer in Quebec, 1933.

Curry, Nory and Doris before the empty house that served as kitchen and studio, Gaspé, 1934.

Peter and Bobs Haworth
in Haliburton.

Walter Fraser, 1933.

Introducing summer students to the world of puppetry at
Central Technical School.

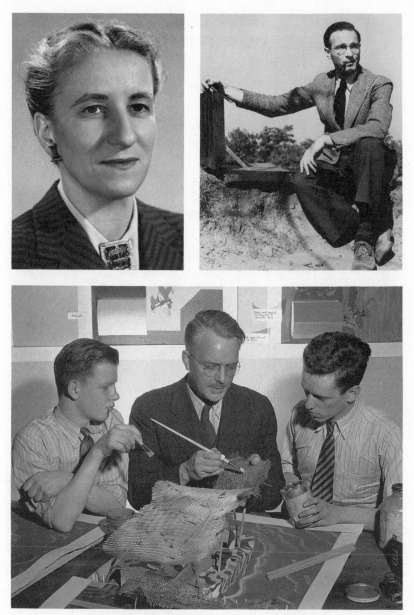

Art Department colleagues at Central Tech: Virginia Luz, Charles Goldhamer, and Dawson Kennedy, here giving a lesson in camouflage to war-time students. *(Goldhamer photo courtesy of the E.P. Taylor Reference Library, Art Gallery of Ontario, Toronto)*

En route to England aboard the *American Farmer*. Left to right: Maurice Birchall ("Winnipeg"), the Major, Elinor Christie, Nory, and Doris, September 1935.

The Iron Jelloids: Nory, George, and Doris, 1936.

Ted and Elizabeth Acheson with Gunther, 1936.

Winter painting in Haliburton, 1937. Left to right: Virginia
Luz, Curry, and Doris.

The compleat painter: Doris in the Gaspé, 1944.

Fool's Paradise, April 1942: "a little white box of a house with a blue roof... looking as if the first strong wind would blow it away."

Roofing the garage addition, 1946.

The Girl with the Jeep, loaded with flowers and canvases, 1950. *(Photo by Ken Bell)*.

Fool's Paradise, complete with angel weather-vane, 1950. *(Photo by Ken Bell)*.

11

Changing Colours

THE PROSPECT OF TEACHING full-time at Central Tech made me reluctant to spend the holidays directing camps. I needed time to be an artist, and Curry's father said we could use his hunting shack at North Lake to live in for the summer if we wanted to. It was about eighteen miles from Haliburton, very isolated, hard to reach and a bit rough, but Curry was keen, and I was thrilled at the thought of two whole months to paint with no other responsibilities. Curry's brother Ronald prophesied that we'd be frightened to death when we were left in the woods by ourselves, good for about two nights, but we refused to be put off. Mother almost had a fit and was sure that we would be attacked by a bear, lost in the bush, stricken with appendicitis, or raped and murdered, probably all four.

Curry's Uncle Andy and his wife, Jennie, came with us to help carry our gear and see us settled. We had to

take enough panels, canvases, and other art supplies for
two months, as well as basic food supplies, clothes, and
bedding. Andy's car was a Model T Ford, with a high
frame that could clear the rock outcroppings and deep
ruts on the backwoods lumber road that led to the first
lake. It was advanced in age; when we came to a hill, we
all piled out to lighten the load, and sometimes to push
the car up. Once at the lake, Andy unloaded the outboard
motor he had brought and then hauled a skiff out of the
underbrush where it lay hidden. It was a five-mile trip
along the shore of this uninhabited lake, five miles of
woods and more woods, with only a lily-clogged bay or a
bare rocky promontory as a landmark.

Andy had a woodsman's eyes. He could see the entrance to the portage where we saw only unbroken forest.
He safe-stored the skiff and its motor, and we heaved the
first load onto our backs and started up the trail. For a
long mile and a half we trudged uphill through bush over
the height of land to North Lake, then back for the rest
of the gear. Andy was long and lean with a leisurely
loose-limbed gait that we could just keep up to. His blue
eyes twinkled when he called a rest stop, and we all threw
our packs and ourselves against a tree trunk and enjoyed
his kidding. Jennie was a small round woman with a
gentle smile and little to say, but game for her share of the
load. At the end of the portage there was a rowboat
hidden in the trees to take us across the lake. On the far
shore we could see Mr. Curry's hunting shack, which
stood on a point of land above some shelving rocks that
made a natural dock.

It was a two-room hunting cabin: a kitchen with a

woodstove, a rough plank table, and one bunk; the second room with rows of bunks down each side, enough beds for a whole hunting party. We left Andy and Jennie the privacy of the kitchen and chose places for ourselves in the other room under the windows that looked out to the lake.

The next day I wrote: "Tin plates are laid out on the table, potatoes are boiling in the big pot and beans in the frying pan. Jennie is just about to plunge into *The Outline of History*. Andy has vanished into parts unknown, and beyond the door is our lake. Thirty slender pines are outside one window and through the other I can see the wooded hill across the water. Slim little Curry is cutting bread, comic from the back in her dark blue jeans with the scarlet bandanna hanging from her pocket and her limp green sun-hat on top. This morning Andy took us down the shore, and in the reeds ahead we saw a moving red spot that became a deer, and we got close enough to watch her shaking the flies away, moving about feeding on the lily pads. Then when we were close, she raised her head, looked long at us, turned, and in great graceful plunges cleared the weeded spot, then turned for another look before she disappeared into the woods."

Andy and Jennie stayed for two days, taking us through the short portages to show us the other lakes in the chain. In every lake or pond Mr. Curry had stowed a canoe or rowboat to serve the hunting parties he guided for in the fall. He had given us a big world to live in that summer. We went single file, Andy ahead, his pack moving in rhythm with his legs and his gun held loosely but in readiness. Curry walked lightly, hat perched perilously

on the side of her head above her hank of dark hair and
the silly red handkerchief swinging with each step. Jennie plodded along behind me.

The next day we ferried Andy and Jennie across early,
and left them at the portage, exulting that now we were
alone on our own lake. "Then round the shore we idled,
discovering a loon's nest with one egg, a new warbler, a
pitcher plant, a glorious rocky height, the creek's mouth,
and so home.

"As we were working away at the big table in the
afternoon Curry heard a splash, and we jumped up to see
a whole family of ducks, marshalled by the mother. They
sailed past, diving, aeroplaning, swimming, until she
herded them out onto a rock where they all shook and
preened and fussed and finally settled down, all nine of
them in a row. At dinner time we made a birthday party
for me with candles and muffins and coffee and a sense
of high occasion."

For the first two days that we were on our own, we
made sure that we had done all our chores before dark,
including our last visit to the extraordinary privy. This
consisted of two slim saplings nailed between trees to
make a seat that was suspended over a natural crevice in
the floor of the woods. Privy was the wrong word for it,
but it was an airy, leafy retreat in fine weather. Before
dark fell, we were safe indoors, with a lamp lit. By our
third day we felt at home, far too comfortable with our
woods, our shore, our sylvan perch out back, to be uneasy
when night came. Our delight was to take the boat and
creep in it along the shore at dusk, seeing how close we
could get to the loons that shared the lake with us, and
hoping our deer would be feeding again.

We painted and drew, and drew and painted. We were up as soon as the sun woke us, dropping into the water for a quick wake-up dip and a more leisurely bath squatting in the warmth of the sun. Sometimes without putting on any clothes we built a fire at the shore and made our tea there, and carried it to the table strung between the trees to have with breakfast. Chores next. Andy had left us a supply of split wood, but there was the washing-up, beds to tidy, water to carry from the lake, ourselves to dress for work and the sketch boxes to get ready, squeezing out the colours, loading a couple of panels, making sure we had turps, rags, matches, emergency rations and our raincoats with us. Sometimes we went by boat to the far shore to find a place to paint. Sometimes we went off through the woods, and then I carried the .22 rifle and some bullets in my pocket in case we should meet a partridge.

The shores of North Lake were wooded with second growth almost to the water's edge. The challenge was to find a subject among so much sameness. It taught me to see subtle variations in the greens, from the bluer green of the pines to the lighter and yellower green of the birch and poplar. Skies were always changing. I learned the difference between cumulus and cirrus clouds and how to describe the tones of the night sky, with stars or in moonlight, and one memorable night after rain I saw a moon-bow and painted it. There was a small bay covered with lily pads, and the undersides of the floating leaves ranged from crimson to orange-yellow, which showed when the wind turned them over. The movement of the water and the reflections of rock and trees were worth hours of study and endless attempts. Sometimes Curry

and I went off together, sometimes separately. We tacked
our sketches up on the sun-tanned wooden walls of the
cabin and lived with them, discovering weaknesses that
we could correct and occasionally virtues that reassured
us.

"July 10: This morning, eating porridge by our lovely
out-of-doors fire on our log stools, we discovered that
instead of Saturday it was Sunday, and we had skipped
a day. Tomorrow we shall have been here a week –
impossible as it seems. Already home seems very remote,
and Tech just doesn't exist. It's been a stormy noon. Rain
and wild wind came just after dinner and we abandoned
the dishes to draw the lake. Yesterday was good. We
woke up to bright sunshine and trekked over to Beaver
Pond for a morning's work in the lily pads, then dinner,
cooked dirtily but blissfully among the ants on a nice
rocky point, and wonderful clouds to tantalize us, till they
began thundering and sprinkling. Home we dashed, hysterical with laughter, and dragged our bedding indoors
and then danced in the rain, and finally went in for a
swim. The day before yesterday I found myself comfortably settled beside a very yellow and green serpent with
a bright vermilion tongue. It gave me an uncomfortable
morning."

We depended on each other as models and made fre-
quent drawings and many caricatures. Many of the latter
we sent off to family and friends as light-hearted illustrations of our life together. Curry was lithe and slim but
with beautifully feminine hips, which I delighted to exaggerate. "I wrote all morning to Mother and M and
sketched Curry between times. Never shall I forget the
sight she made on her way to photograph our ducks,

camouflaged, walking on all fours in the flapping grey
flannel nightgown and her little khaki behind sticking out
the back." On our occasional overnight ventures to East
Lake we carried all our living and working gear on our
backs. I staggered under the pack, with my bird glasses
around my neck and my gun in my hands. Curry, far more
picturesque, was burdened with the red blanket, rolled
and around her neck, rubber boots tied to that, then two
canvases hanging down her back, from one shoulder a
sketch box, under her arm her huge portfolio, and in her
hand two paddles.

Looking back on that summer, I think its greatest gift
was silence. Curry is a person of few words. She has never
just chattered. In time, we came to read through meals,
eating at the table outdoors, our books propped against
the trees that supported the table. We had brought some
solid reading with us. Besides Wells's *The Outline of History*
we had Durant's *The Story of Philosophy*, a saga of several
generations of a theatrical family called *Broom Stages*, and
Kristin Lavransdatter by Sigrid Undset. We had no radio.
If a leaf fell, we heard it and looked to see why. Every
sound meant something.

Mail was an event, brought to us by the rare fishing
party that passed through. For me, it was usually painful.
Mother had little sympathy with my retreat into the
wilderness. "I do understand how she feels but I wish she
had some imagination. For all she loves, she can never
understand, and, with Virgil, 'One grows tired of everything except understanding.' I think I'll just try to forget
her in between mails. M writes from London this time,
and says we must come to England together, and my heart
says yes, we must! Surely if we will we can. But my mind

says, next time it will be with her family and you know it.
We've just chased a huge mouse down his hole. A porcu-
pine is chewing up the rowboat, and far out on the
glimmering moonlit lake a loon is crying. Tonight is a true
star night. 'The sky has a thousand eyes,' but we are tired
and beds are too inviting to be ignored."

We went to East Lake one evening and spent an hour
in excited curiosity and trepidation, watching a moose
from the canoe and making sketches of him. We stayed
until it was too dark to see him, then paddled on to a little
island to make camp in the dark and get ourselves a
much-needed supper. "Such a falling over, such a spilling,
such a losing of knives and dropping of butter and choking on pine smoke, and crying of damns, and intense
enjoyment, all in one meal. Then we paddled down the
shore, and it was eerie. The flash would make the nearby
snags startlingly bright and the shore secretive and black.
The big dead spruce hanging over the water was a feath-
ery vision, as unreal as a dream and as isolated."

A merganser duck with a single duckling was very shy
when she first used to pass our point, skittering quickly
past and clucking to the baby to hurry up, but she had
become accustomed to us and swam by two or three times
a day without concern. The baby, now a teen-ager, was
in a panic the first time that his mother left him alone on
the lake. He spent all day skimming up and down calling
to her. We saw her in the sky, returning, and watched him
aeroplane towards her, crying, as she glided down beside
him. The next day he was less upset, and after a few days
he would fish happily by himself while she was away.

One day a flock of blue jays came by, and Curry said
it was a sign that summer was almost over. The calendar

was saying the same thing, but the end came abruptly with a letter in Mother's handwriting, marked IMPOR-TANT. Suddenly the peace was shattered and I was under orders to get home right away for half a dozen important reasons, including visits from my brothers with their families. Andy and Jennie came back to help us break camp.

"Night of the 25th: It has been such a queer day. The morning woke me early, silently, to idle morning thoughts, interrupted by the little merganser, and I watched him swimming along in his young lovely pride, looking lonely. He has been so sweet lately. He stands up in the water and flaps his small wings, and then splashes about after little fish, and this morning he caught one just by the rock, and at that, I heard Andy go out, and I watched with fresh pride as the duck wasn't startled, and I was glad he trusted us so, and I wondered where his mother was, all before lying down again. A few minutes later I heard the .22 pop, and I decided that if the porcu-pine who had been gnawing at the boat were being cornered I should be on deck. So out I hustled in my bathing suit, and Andy, to my horror, was shooting at our dear little duck, and even before I spoke he shot again, and I saw the lovely little thing turn over, and then choking with tears and dismay I climbed over the rock to him, and he was a poor little dead thing in my hands."

The return from North Lake was like dropping from paradise into hell. Everyone talking at once. Noise. Con-fusion. Chaos. Doug and Audrey and the baby had come south on holiday from Kapuskasing, and Ken and Betty and two-year-old Brian were in Toronto for the Canadian National Exhibition, staying down the street at the

Caswells'. There were constant family gatherings and trips to the CNE, and although I loved them all, I couldn't stand to be in the middle of it. Even the return to school was a relief.

12

Fresh Perspectives

THE ONTARIO TRAINING COLLEGE for Technical Teachers – quite a mouthful – was a typically government-style red brick building next door to the Hamilton Technical School. In it were gathered the would-be teachers of printing, sheet-metal work, carpentry, motor mechanics, and so on – about twenty men – and a half-dozen young women who were, most of them, being trained to teach domestic science, a euphemism for cooking and dressmaking. Two of us were qualifying to teach art. We were a conscientious group, getting along well together, doing our best to support the poor victim whose turn it was to teach us a practice lesson, and spending our spare time in riotous games of badminton in the big room upstairs.

John Byers and I, both graduates of the Ontario College of Art, stayed at the same boarding house a few blocks from the school, being thoroughly spoiled. Our landlady, Mrs. Jones, was not only a good cook, she had an eye, and every dish was as attractive to see as to taste. Three times a day we sat down to a small feast. I relished my first year of living away from home.

At the college the lectures were elementary to anyone who had done much reading or thinking about education, as I had at leadership camps and for my own CGIT group. The real challenge for me came in the practice teaching. Hortense Gordon was my critic-teacher. At the time I didn't know that she was a highly respected abstract artist, one of the pioneers of that movement in Canada. We liked each other, and she gave me her theories of design to teach, with the flattering comment that she would not usually trust anyone else to handle them.

Her analyses of the principles of design were far ahead of anything that I had been offered at the College of Art. There, although Herbert Stansfield offered us a nodding acquaintance with Jay Hammond's science of dynamic symmetry, we had been taught little theory. Usually we were given an assignment, a lampshade to design, a repeating pattern to make up, and praised or criticized on the details as we worked them out. We had far too little experience to arrive at our own generalizations. I was hungry for more intellectual content, and Mrs. Gordon provided it. She taught that the basic principle of rhythm was orderly sequential change: of direction, as by allowing the trunks of trees in a grove to vary subtly in their slope from the vertical; of size, as by making sure that a group of boulders in the foreground of a painting included small, medium, and large, with no two exactly the same size; of form, by using several intermediate shapes between a circle and a long rectangle; of tone, by letting the intermediate greys be in even steps between black and

white, and so on with colour and texture. Any two elements in a design could be brought into harmony by
creating a step half-way between them. To me, this was
light shining into darkness.

Her husband was the director of the art department of
the technical school where she taught and supervised my
practice teaching. I believe that he was a heavy drinker.
It is the kindest explanation of the rudeness with which
he treated her in public. He would burst into the classroom without knocking and ridicule her or scold her
about some trifle. Poor Mrs. Gordon maintained a tense
little smile and made no protest, implying to the class and
to me that John was just being facetious. But the pulse
in her throat throbbed more noticeably.

Back in Toronto, change was neither rhythmic nor
orderly. When Doug and Audrey had returned to
Kapuskasing after their holiday at home, they were
greeted by a dismissal notice. The company was laying
off staff and Doug had been there only two years. They
had allowed him to come south and buy major house
furnishings with no warning of what lay ahead. It was a
blow. Mother rose to the occasion with characteristic
generosity and invited them to move back home until
Doug could find a new job.

Equally characteristic was Mother's inability to carry
her generosity into her relations with them. She was
critical and difficult, keeping Audrey on the defensive,
and the mounting tensions between them naturally involved Doug. Mercifully, eight-month-old Dale was too
young to be considered naughty, whatever he did, but he
was a lively, restless baby and inevitably disruptive.

I would arrive home from Hamilton on Friday night,

too late for the family meal. Mother would keep my
dinner in the oven and bring it to me at the dining-room
table, where she would season it with her tale of the woes
of the week. I remember held-over white fish, held-over
white potatoes and cauliflower or creamed onions, with
an obbligato of Grandmother's unreasonableness,
Grandfather's stubbornness, Dale's being spoilt by Audrey who spent all her time fussing over him instead of
helping with the house, and Doug's futile approach to
job-hunting by sending off applications instead of chasing
around and seeing people. Poor Mother. She had no way
of imagining what it was like for them, and no tolerance
of their differences of temperament. I was her safety
valve, and she blew off steam to me all through my
miserable meal.

The climax came at Christmas, when Doug's gift to his
young wife was black lace lingerie. I thought it was rather
touching that the poor lad had not had all the romance
knocked out of him yet, but Mother exploded. Driving
back to Hamilton after the winter holiday was pure
pleasure.

The office secretary at the training school had offered me
a blind date for the dance that closed the fall term, and so
I met Walter Fraser. He was eight years older than I and
serious about finding himself a wife, and although I
wanted marriage too, I was in no hurry. Mother had been
told by a plausible fortune-teller that I was to marry a
university professor when I was twenty-six, which gave
me four years still to play around. But I liked Walt and

enjoyed his attentions, even while I doubted that he was for me the ultimate answer.

Marjorie was teaching at the Ontario Ladies' College at Whitby, and we saw each other on weekends and talked long hours about love, and what it meant, and what it did not mean. During that year she began to realize that she really did care for Roy, who had been pursuing her faithfully for three years.

"M and I dined yesterday lovingly, if such an adverb isn't ridiculous, and it was as it always is, completely natural and easy to be with her again. Later, in her room, she talked about Roy to me, and as she sat at her table, hand nervously scribbling on some paper, her eyes on the wall in front, she was a woman, no little girl left at all, and I felt as if I were watching her step truly into grown-up land. It was all a bit like 'our future selves' and it pressed home the truth of our growth. We are women now. I'm so glad Roy has come as he did. Funny how I used to dread the time a man would come between us, and funny how little like that it has seemed. Perhaps if or when M has become 'sure' it may be more so, but I doubt it."

Much of my year in Hamilton was spent in an emotional confusion, trying to sort out my own feelings about Walt, agonizing if a week went by without a telephone call, in highest heaven when he was in attendance, doubting him, doubting myself, dreading Mother's critical appraisal, trying to see him with Marjorie's eyes, being very young and inexperienced, and very much obsessed with sex. Walt was the first person to stimulate that. My diary makes painful reading.

"Oh Walt you are sweet! And I was happy in the movie

with his hand rubbing mine, his other moving on my arm, and I deliberately took his hand and enjoyed having it and took his kisses and returned them gladly – and wanted them! And while I don't suppose that the Big Moment has arrived, yet what fun it's been and is. I love teasing and being teased – and I like you Walt. Good Lord, how much of this drivel am I going to write?" Pages and pages of it. "I think I'll write a magazine about the poor little schoolgirl who got out by herself in New York (Hamilton) where she fell in love with the first man who kissed her (Walt) and mistook his civilities for ardent passion. The fade-out will come when she returns to her native village (Toronto) and he continues his blissful career as a breaker of inexperienced feminine hearts."

This was the first year that I entertained myself by drawing house plans. It was a way of making some of my daydreams concrete. "It's to be one of those lovely old square stone houses, and I'm going to rebuild it inside if necessary till it's just right for us. Walter will have a little den on one side of the front door, with the telephone. The other will be a big living room with a lovely open fireplace. The dining room will be small but very sunny and my kitchen will be utterly compact."

"Friday night. Old habit is strong. I feel dishonest keeping secrets from Marjorie – and tonight I confessed to the precarious position of my heart. Her love is such a steady strong rock in my life. I know it so utterly, that I look with a little fear on any liking that hasn't such a good foundation of long and early friendship. Even if Walter should like me, love me a little, it can't be love for my sake. He doesn't know my weaknesses, my fears and joys and passions and fancies, and I don't know his – and I don't care for him, love him, the way I do my dearest. It's the man-woman factor that changes it all."

The quality of the intimacy that Marjorie and I shared was not at all like that of lovers, more like that of twins. We stood on the same ground, secure in an understanding of each other built over the years, sharing the same ideals, the same sense of humour, the same memories. Our love for each other was not possessive. Each of us wanted the other to marry and have children. We had a respect for the other's talents, an intense caring for the other's richness of life, and a continuing need of the understanding possible between us because of the years of knowing.

I had had one brief obsessive friendship with a fellow camp leader in which I began to recognize a sexual element in her caresses. I was immediately uncomfortable and made sure that there were no further opportunities for any physical expression of our affection. Between Marjorie and me this had never been a factor.

When term was over in Hamilton, and I was safely "certified," there was a precious week before I was due back at Central Tech, time for my promised trip to Moncton to visit Dad's family.

"April 14, 1933: The porter is making up the berth, and I feel a childish delight in the precision with which he pulls down the upper and snaps things into place. Then he slaps up the rings and hangs the curtains. It's exciting to watch. I love the ceremonials of travelling at night, dust bags for my hat, shoes for shining, the smooth round head of the Negro porter, the slow grin of one to the other, crisp cool white sheets spread by the casual but expert black hands. I woke, as I thought, just before dawn, and looked with wonder into a world of water with a lighted city rising high on the other side. Quebec? I think so. It gave me a strange feeling to see it in such an unfamiliar guise. Then a little later I woke again to find snow outside, drifted up around little Quebec houses like so many A.Y. Jackson canvases. Still later there was the broad blue-green St. Lawrence, broken by floating ice, brooding in colour under the grey sky, with a ghost hill on the other side, faintly lighter than the water in its snowy patches, faintly darker where the woods made patterns on it. And in the foreground, rotting drifts, bits of villages, white-washed buildings, or faded red and green. My heart ached to be painting them. We've been passing villages with intriguing little houses that are gone before I can get them down, but at least I'm accumulating a lot of useful scribbles."

In Moncton it was again in the big house on the hill that I stayed. Three of Dad's sisters were living there together. Adelaide, elegant and sardonic, was mistress of the house and of her dead husband's estate. Aunt Molly, the eldest of the family, and the smallest, was her companion. She had been a young teacher, engaged to be married to an equally young clergyman, when Grandmother McCarthy became an invalid after my father's birth. She gave up her marriage to look after her mother and the smaller children. It was she who encouraged Dad to earn the first university degree in the family. She and her young clergyman wrote regularly to each other for the rest of their lives and neither married. Dad felt for her a fierce loyalty, and had taught me to look on her as his real mother. The three sterling-silver dessert spoons that

I cherish and use every day were her Christmas presents to me. We had written back and forth through the years but nothing had prepared me for the diminutive and dynamic old lady who was at that time avidly following the radio broadcasts of the Allan Cup series. Moncton was in the hockey finals, and she knew every player by name.

The third sister, quiet Aunt Fon, lived with the disgrace of her daughter's unmarried pregnancy twenty years before, which was as palpably present as was poor Aunt Fon herself. She spoke very little, a black-garbed ghost, gentle, sweet, responding eagerly to my attempts to be friendly. She took me to meet the disgraced daughter and the seducer who had been compelled to marry her. Roy's belly overhung his pants. His vulgarity was as evident as his curly red hair. Privately I thought him a fat boor, and my heart ached for both women. The illegitimate child, a fine promising lad, I was told, had been killed by a gun accident at sixteen. His mother, faded into middle age, welcomed me and showed me photographs of the boy with obvious pride, but I left with the feeling that neither the present nor the future had any joy in it, and that life was over for her too.

"Saturday morning: I never see old photographs without marvelling at the beautiful woman Mother was. Aunt Molly has some snaps from Vancouver with Doris a square baby and no eyes, Douglas one round grin, and Kenneth a lovely-looking child, with beautiful eyes and a much more sensitive face. But Mother is the loveliest surprise of all. She was beautiful, smooth of contour, and smooth of skin, with a bloom on her as if she were healthy and happy. I felt envy of Dad for his lovely young wife, and his adorable family. Aunt Fon is a sweet person. I find myself liking her best, her patience, and her loving way of remembering us all as children, even her dependence and gentleness, without the spice of Aunt Ad, and without the intelligent grasp that Aunt Molly has kept. She is more like a picture than a person, bent and passive in her chair with the footstool their father had made for them to use as children in church. Her black gown must be twenty years old at least, with jet beads, and silk bands down the front. She takes pride in the old home and its treasures."

Marjorie met me on my return home with the news that now she was "sure" about Roy, and still between us nothing was changed. It was then we began to plan a summer that would give Roy and me a chance to get to know each other. I had regretfully parted with Gabriel and bought myself a full-sized Chev, strong enough to pull the little boat and trailer that I fell for. This was a punt, complete with oars, that could be packed full of gear and pulled behind the car on its own trailer. Roy would sleep in the car, and Curry and Marjorie and I would share an eight-by-eight tent.

It was certainly an educational summer. Roy was an experienced camper, good at fires, at packing, at all the man's jobs that Curry and I were accustomed to doing for ourselves. What we learned was to contain our impatience at the time it took Roy to do those things. Both of us were quick workers and Roy's pace was deliberate. We bit our tongues (usually) and got out the sketchbooks to make use of the minutes. What we all learned was not to leave Marjorie alone with practical problems. The morning that Curry and I were off painting and Roy had taken

the car into town for servicing, we left Marjorie, reason-
ably enough, to get lunch – menu agreed, no worries. But
Marjorie had grown up with an older sister and a mother
who liked cooking, in a doctor's household that always
included a maid, and she was an innocent in a kitchen and
even worse at a campfire. We found her opening our big
five-pound tin of jam not by prying off the lid, but by
cutting it around with a can-opener!

For Curry and me it was a welcome opportunity to
work from material very different from the woods and
water of North Lake. We drove east to Ottawa and then
turned north up into the Gatineau Hills. Quebec villages
were organized differently than our familiar Haliburton,
and the architecture of the houses interested us both. On
the way down from Mont Laurier, our most northerly
point, we saw a frame house of such charm that I stopped
the car, backed up for a better look, and then ventured
through the gate and up to the door to express our interest
and pleasure. We were graciously received. Our French
was equal to the occasion, and we were given a tour of
the interior of "Ensoleillé." It was the memory of that
home with an old church window set in the end wall of
the living room that dominated my house plans from then
on.

We travelled as far east as Baie Saint-Paul, camping,
exploring, and painting until it was time for Marjorie and
Roy to return to Toronto. Mrs. Beer was not willing to
let Marjorie travel overnight with Roy on the train un-
chaperoned, so we drove them back to Montreal to catch
a day train home. Then Curry and I, having stashed the
punt and trailer in my cousin's yard in Saint-Lambert,
took off along the south shore towards the Gaspé penin-

sula. Without its load the car was winged. We tented
wherever we could find a little stream and a good view,
often on private property. We would knock at the house
and ask to have our water pot filled, and if we liked the
person who came to the door, we would then ask permission to camp beside the stream. Curry was great at spying
out fresh vegetables in the garden and inspiring small
boys to go catch brook trout for our breakfast. I remember one day when the heavens had opened and the rain
was coming down in torrents, and from the driver's seat
I watched little Curry, in rubber boots and her volumi-
nous yellow slicker, her rain hat dripping all around,
holding up her fire-blackened pot and asking, "Avez-
vous un peu de l'eau, s'il vous plaît?"

This was during the Depression and before the baby
bonus, and the people of the Gaspé were very poor. There
was no paint for the shabby little houses. But the fishing
boats and dories had to be painted for their very survival,
and the odd bits of colour left over were used on doors or
window frames. Sea-silvered wood, with touches of faded
blue and pink and green, in a setting of breath-taking
grandeur! No wonder we fell in love with it.

Among other accomplishments of the summer was
falling out of love with Walt. "I've been rereading my
spring weekends with Walter, marvelling now that I am
utterly without desire. I don't want to be kissed at all. I
am bored at the thought of physical intimacy, and all I
want to do is work and have men around as friends. All
the virtue claimed by psychologists for sublimation seems
to have been proved true by the summer. Marrying Walt
seems just an amusing idea."

In January Walt told me that he was engaged to be

married, and I was able to rejoice for him sincerely, and to observe with interest that as soon as Walter was no longer courting me, Mother thought he was a "lovely boy."

"September 1933: All week I've been feeling like an artist. Peter [Haworth] and Charlie [Goldhamer] liked my sketches, assured me that I'd learn more at my stage from working by myself than by studying at a summer school, and Charles (Oh heavenly joy) said, 'I've always thought that some day you would be one of our more important painters.'"

The art department at Central Tech was on the fourth floor, strung along a corridor that crossed the centre of the building, above the auditorium. This corridor was several steps higher than the rest of the fourth floor, isolated, with a precious sense of privacy. At last I rated a room of my own and was spared having classes up in the life room, or down on the ground floor. A single sink in an alcove served the whole corridor, and since almost all of our work involved paint and therefore water, that sink was like the village well in Biblical times. Students and teachers met there and waited in turn to reach an arm through the crowd to the tap. Gossip thrived. I am sure this was one of the reasons for the comfortable, informal atmosphere of the department. Peter, who could be authoritarian when he chose, was a clown, unable to resist an audience. Dawson Kennedy, fresh from a degree at the Royal College of Art in London, was gifted in tongues; he could mimic any of the accents he had met in England, and did. We had a lot of fun, some of it at the expense of

those of the academic teachers who were baffled by our
nonsense. I remember affectionately the sweet woman
who taught French, and who never did get the point of
the riddle "What happens to a girl who wears cotton
stockings?" to which the correct answer was "Nothing."

"February 27: I went in to tell Nory something, and
Peter came in and sat on the table with us, looking very
nice in his Harris tweed – I wiped off the table for him
with pink Kleenex. He started in to tell us all about the
war, learning to fly, going up in his first balloon flight, his
terror, and throwing out the sand and pulling in the valve.
It was easy and casual and companionable, and we could
just see him strutting about London in his very new
breeks. He is a naughty man. He met Jean Blundell [of
the academic staff] in the hall at noon and when she said,
'Your wife looked beautiful last night,' he pretended to be
surprised and said, 'Well that's funny. She's not usually
considered good-looking at all. *I'm* thought to be the
handsome one of the family.'"

Peter encouraged his teachers to exhibit in the juried
shows. The formal openings of these exhibitions of the
major Canadian art societies were the dressiest and most
crowded events in the art gallery's year. There would be
two thousand people thronging into the building. The
societies vied with one another to attract the biggest VIPs
to make the opening speeches. Vice-regal luminaries
came and were entertained beforehand at formal dinners.
In the exhibition of each society, the president's painting,
a major work, was given pride of place on the south wall
of the long room, where it could be seen from the main
entrance.

Artists who were represented in the show were allowed in the day before, on Varnishing Day, so called from the nineteenth-century practice of touching up a recently finished painting. Varnishing Day was a chance to see where your work was hung, to digest the significance of a place in the octagonal gallery (for the avant-garde) or stuck in a corner (where it wouldn't show too much), or off in the square gallery with the water-colours and left-overs. Centre wall in one of the long galleries was a prize! Early arrival on opening night was rewarded with a seat in the sculpture court, a chance to watch in comfort the procession of the great ones arriving from Grange House and taking their places on the platform. We wore our most formal gowns, enjoying the drama of the floor-length sweeping skirts, the bared backs and modestly suggested bosoms. I realized what was in the little Pre-vocational's mind when she wrote on an exam paper in the health department that the function of the skin was to "cover the bones and make you more formal."

"March 1934: After my fourth OSA opening as an exhibitor and my first OSA dinner party, with Peter and Mrs. Haworth, Dawson Kennedy and his fiancée Kathleen Cooley, recently arrived from England, Charles, Nory, Ed [Noffke, of OCA], and M [Roy was teaching in Grimsby]. It was really a very nice party, dinner by candlelight, gentlemen all dressed, ladies ditto, place cards made by the Pre-vocationals, a thoroughly good dinner. Mother bought a new set of dishes in honour of the occasion. I wished we could have sat around in our lovely living room all evening. Somehow I felt Peter's approval and I warmed to it."

After Easter, I completed the move into my new studio, the big cellar room that I had been allowed to take over, to line with wallboard, and to glorify by painting the concrete floor turquoise and the brick fireplace a greyed pink. The windows were small and high, but I was used to painting at night and so grateful for the space and privacy that I had no complaints.

Marjorie's wedding was set for June, as soon as term was over, and her sister Eleanor and I were to be brides-maids. Marjorie shocked her mother by insisting on being married on a Monday morning, an impossible time for caterers and florists. But it was the first day the licence could be ready and it gave Marjorie and Roy the after-noon to drive north to our cabin in Muskoka for their first few days of honeymoon and rest before taking off on a camping trip to the west coast.

The service is memorable to me especially for the moment when they exchanged the vows – not, as was usual, by repeating them phrase by phrase after the minister, but without prompting, clearly, in one unbroken pledge. I was unprepared for that and the tears sprang. Another poignant moment came after the formalities of signing the register, when Marjorie's father held out his hand for the completed marriage certificate, and the minister said, "Not any longer, Dr. Beer. It's somebody else's business to look after her now."

While the bride and groom were driving west with their tent, Curry and Nory and I were off to explore the Maritimes with ours. We had heard so much about Peggy's Cove that we made it our objective. But the area around Peggy's is impossible tenting country. There isn't a bush on the landscape! We drove as far south as

Lunenburg looking for something as good to paint and as hospitable for tenting as the coast of the Gaspé, but we looked in vain. We turned around and headed back to the country we had discovered the year before. It was even better than our memory of it.

We pitched the tent on a ledge of rough red rock ten feet above the beach that shelved down past the tide wrack to the salt Atlantic. Away off to the right we could see Percé Rock jutting out beyond the high cliffs of the headland. Behind us, sloping gently up to the road, our big field was a garden of daisies and slender blue iris. A tactful grove of spruce near the tent gave us the essential privacy. The family who owned the field included Maurice, a young man who took one look at Nory and became our host, friend, escort, encyclopaedia, and personal lobster-poacher. With his help, we located the owner of the empty house a few hundred yards down the road and succeeded in renting it for five dollars for the season. It took another five dollars to secure a workable woodstove for its kitchen, but that was all we needed. We used the house as studio and kitchen, and slept in the tent, in heaven.

We did most of our painting at Barachois, a fishing village nearby. A daily train ambled along a sandbar that curved towards Barachois and climbed over a bridge across the channel that emptied the river into the sea. The bridge was high enough to let the two-masted fishing boats pass under it into the harbour. Perching on the edge of this railway bridge gave a perfect view of the little boats tethered in the channel or tied to the stages along the shore. Behind them lay the mud flats of the river mouth, stretching away to the blue hills in the distance.

When supper was over and we were strolling up the
road to the post office with Maurice or one or two of the
other young swains, we would hear the slow putt-putt-
putt of the one-stroke engines and see the fishing boats
putting out to sea for a night of drifting for herring. After
dark we would see only their lanterns and hear the
putt-putt. All night they drifted for bait. In the morning,
far out at sea, the nets were pulled in, and each herring
was hooked on the end of a line which was lowered into
the depths where the cod lurked. When the cod had been
hauled up and all the bait was gone, the fishermen headed
for home, this time under sail. From early afternoon until
five or six o'clock the ships, leaning before the strong
afternoon breeze, sails sparkling in the sunlight, came
dancing in on the white-capped blue waves. As they drew
close to the bridge, down tumbled the sails, and the little
two-masters would be brought smoothly to their moor-
ings at the stages and tied up for unloading.

I spent hours drawing the men gutting the cod, watching the rhythmic movement of their mittened hands and
the sweep of the knife, and listening to their gentle voices
teasing one another about having their portraits painted.

The social life was almost too active. Tall, dark, and
handsome Earl Roberts, who worked at the store, had
reacted normally to Nory, and was around a great deal.
Astonishingly, he gradually transferred his attentions to
me and made my days and evenings sing. The Anglican
minister was a young man who wanted the young people
to play together but to behave themselves. There were
lively square dances in the church hall, with plenty of
noise and music, but a minimum of rowdiness and drink.
Earl swung me round and round until I reeled and could

see nothing but the glint of his black eyes. Cliff, who also worked at the store and was a beautiful dancer, was also glad of three new women in the village. He used to take Nory riding behind him on his motorcycle. We worked and played hard that summer.

In the car driving back from the Gaspé, Nory and I began to wish that we could go off to study where we would really learn more about painting. This was the first seed of our dream of a year away from home and teaching, which grew all winter and flowered late in 1935.

13

Major Discoveries

GRANDMOTHER HAD DIED while we were still exploring the Maritimes. By the time Mother's letter reached me the funeral was over, and her death would have remained very distant and unreal to me except for Grandpa's letter. Grandmother had been increasingly difficult during her last year. Hardening of the arteries was the answer Dr. Beer gave to explain her irrational spells. Sometimes she diappeared from the house and went up to Mrs. Trowell with stories of the cruelties practised on her by Mother and Grandpa. They were devastated by her inventions. I imagined that her death would be a relief to Grandpa. How naïve and wrong I was!

"My Dearest Doris: Thank you dear for your kind and sympathetic letter of the 22nd. I have been so prostrated with grief that I have been hardly able to concentrate my mind on anything much less write to anyone since I came home from Lévis where I received a most cordial and sympathetic welcome and tender and loving care from my dear sister, now the last of my own blood. Even now when I call up in my mind that dreadful and tragic hour between six and seven on Friday the 7th when I held my dear little woman in my arms trying to soften her cruel pains, I feel the same helpless despair and horror as I did then waiting alone for the doctor to come with morphia so as to ease her agony. She soon got relief from it but never again uttered a word or gave any sign of consciousness.

"It is quite true dear that few can realize the strong love that is engendered by a lifetime of close intimacy even if one's natures are not tuned to perfect harmony. Of recent years she was unhappy due principally to disappointed dreams of a different life and a growing change of mutuality due to high blood pressure and old age, which is inevitable with undernourished old people. Your uncle and I fully understood this and I for one never resented anything she said or did to me, knowing fully that she was not responsible. For Doris dear I loved her dearly with a love that was the very root of my life and I shall miss her every hour of the day and dream of her at night. She died at 3:30 on Saturday morning, and every night since, I awake from sleep at that hour . . . Excuse this rambling letter. I am not myself at all. God bless you dear, Your affectionate Grandfather."

He was an affectionate grandfather and a congenial friend. We were fortunate to have each other, both of us somewhat wary of Mother, but able to laugh together at the things we could not change.

At last I had several classes of art students on my timetable, even one third-year group. I felt more reconciled to teaching. "This summer has made a difference in

my secret poise. Nothing can give me self-confidence and
assurance like a little love affair. Earl was good for me."

Roy had landed a teaching job in Brampton, and he
and Marjorie had moved into an upstairs flat in an old
brick house there, with a niece of Aunt Nell Baskerville
as their landlady. "September 8: Wednesday night I went
out to Brampton. It was both very happy and a little sad.
Funny to be saying good night to Marjorie and leaving
her, while she shared with Roy the routine of going to bed
that we had done together so often. Funny to realize that
now the closest things were things that were none of my
business, and that even as I didn't tell her the important
things about Earl and me, so she would never tell me the
important things because they wouldn't be just hers to
tell. Perhaps telling isn't very important." Something I
didn't write into my diary was my reaction at being met
by Marjorie in an apron. I hooted with laughter. From
then on, I hardly ever saw her out of it. M took to
domesticity late but with a whole heart.

One of the things I could tell her and talk over was the
idea of a year off to study. It was a vague dream at this
stage. I wanted to go overseas. France was where all the
artists I read about had gone to study, and Paris was
supposed to be the centre of the modern action. But in
spite of having gone to extension courses in French
conversation for two years at U of T, I was afraid of not
understanding French well enough to study in it. Peter
and Dawson and Kath Cooley had all gone to school in
London and were loud in praise of the Royal College of
Art there. Nory had more faith in New York for offering
the latest and best. She and I had many discussions of the
pros and cons without reaching agreement, until she had

the inspiration to suggest a compromise: four months in New York, to England at Christmas for study in London for six months, and then a tour of England in a cheap car. Peter agreed to support our request for leave, without pay of course, and we tightened our discipline of saving every cent we could scrape together. We anticipated needing about two thousand dollars each. I began painting watercolours of bouquets of flowers and found a ready market among Mother's friends. We gave up all luxuries, even the after-school cup of coffee on Bloor Street. Every penny was hoarded.

That spring Mother found Grace, a pretty blonde teen-ager, who needed a job and could actually keep house to Mother's standards. Grace and Grandfather took to each other at once, which freed Mother wonderfully. I was grateful for someone to laugh and sing about the house after the grim years just past. I could go away with an easier mind.

September saw Nory and me off to New York. After a day and a night on the bus, we were landed in the big city in the silent dawn. We found a hole-in-the-wall café where the white enamel tables were less remarkable than the conversation of the other early customers. Pure Brooklynese.

Three days later, having visited the art schools on our list and seen the work done by their students, we were in the dumps. Our own classes at Central Tech were producing work of a much higher standard. What was the point of trying to pull ourselves up by those bootstraps? We decided to head for England at once.

"SS *American Farmer*, September 27, 1935: En route to
England. In bunk, Nory above me – my little light on –
gardenias and roses, gladioli and peonies in riotous confusion, and a warm pain in the heart because people have
been so very very kind. We left for the boat in a feverish
rush, barely taking time to pin our gardenias in place, and
getting unpacked was rather hectic in such a tiny state-
room in steaming heat, but from the moment the boat
moved away from the dock it was sheer joy. The skyline
was just as thrilling as the pictures of it, and the day was
one of quiet greys that made it majestic instead of garish.
Even Liberty was glorified by lovely tones. The breeze
was life-giving. All day I had despaired of ever being cool
again.

"The bath steward turned up all warm smiles and
beams, and assurance that we 'two little girls' could have
our baths any time we jolly well liked. And in no time he
was back with three boxes for me, yellow roses from my
CGIT group, gorgeous flowers from Mother, and candies
too, and he followed us on deck with a corsage for Nory
(also from my Shawnees) – and then I did find the grey
distance blurring a bit because it was so extra sweet of
them. They are darlings."

It was the beginning of one of those separate and
perfect times that life surprises one with. The *American
Farmer* was a freighter that sailed from New York to
London with accommodation for about fifty passengers.
It was single class, without the lavish luxury of first class
on the big liners, but with a much more relaxed and
friendly atmosphere. All the cabins were outside, with
portholes, and the day began with tea delivered to us in
bed. Morning soup and afternoon tea were served on

deck. The top deck was clear for deck chairs and games, the one below offered an adequate promenade. Going round and round that circuit at a brisk pace soon developed our sea legs. Being put at the captain's table for meals made us feel approved and gave us the companionship of the most charming man on board, Major Arthur Balbernie, a well-travelled writer, very British but in love with New York, and delighted to have Nory and me in love with him. Then there was Robert "Scotty" Watson, a young man who had gone to the States seven years earlier and made good but now wanted his five-year-old daughter to grow up a Scottish lass; he was on his way home to prepare the way for his wife and the bairn to follow. Add to that mix Maurice Birchall – whom we called "Winnipeg" – good-looking, callow, and smitten by Nory from the first glimpse; and Elinor Christie from Rhode Island, a very pleasant girl, tall, fair, well built, of about our age. The six of us played deck tennis, danced in the bar at night, sat long hours talking in twos or threes watching the "phosphorescent green froth along the hull and the wide swash behind."

We rode out two days of wild wind and heaving sea, and another day of violent emotional stress because Nory had been flirting with a sailor who was trying to set up a date with her. "Winnipeg went into a dudgeon first of all and then, with his heart in his mouth, he told Nory for the good of her soul about how indiscreet it would be to keep the date – what a hell of a swell girl she was, and he was afraid she might do something to cheapen herself in the eyes of the crew or the passengers. Then he had a perfect spasm of nerves, and walked round and round with me just wringing his hands mentally, while Nory and

the Major went round and round in front of us and the
Major told her the story of his life and about his short
stories sold to the American magazines, and his hope of
getting a novel published."

We were shocked back to a sense of proportion by the
news that Mussolini had bombed some town in
Abyssinia, that Italian troops were mobilizing, and that it
was virtually a declaration of war. We assumed that the
League of Nations would act immediately against Italy.
The Major was in the reserve army, subject to immediate
call-up. He took it for granted that he would be in it.
Winnipeg was excited and talked about "doing his bit for
the old sod" until I could hardly bear it. It was like living
through a replay of novels I had read about the early days
of the First World War. Had we learned nothing?

"When the Major came and sat down I asked him,
'How are you feeling tonight?' and his 'Bloody!' was the
perfect answer." Why – why – why? Nobody *wants* war.
The league was supposed to keep it from ever getting to
this point.

The seriousness of the situation flung us into an intimacy that was very different from the casual friendliness
we had been enjoying. "The Major's fourth campaign,
and he says that life has already been so glorious and he
has known such happiness and also such unhappiness
that if war comes it will be an escape, a way out without
any 'housemaid stuff,' and to hear a grand person like him
saying that makes it all more unbearable than ever. Thank
God for him to talk to, only why must he say he's glad his
last week has been such fun, and that leaving out today,
we must make the memories fit to last four years. Damn
him. Why must he say things like that? But it's true. We

must. If only we could make these days worth keeping."

"Friday October 4: Reports this morning confirmed last night's rumour, 1,700 or 1,800 killed in Abyssinia, men, women, and children, Italy advancing. Baldwin's address expected hourly. There was a queer minute or two in the lounge after dinner, when I came in and found a group of perhaps ten people in front of the radio, all standing, all watching and listening with hushed attention, cigarettes forgotten, and only the man's voice, English and cold, telling us that the league was meeting in committee at that moment to consider steps in Abyssinia.

"This morning gave me another of those perfect hours that seem to come on shipboard with double intensity and frequency. Suddenly the dread left me and I felt great wells of love for England, sympathy with her greatness, and reverence for her poetry. I was sick with need of words to say it. Rupert Brooke helped in the scrappy bits I could remember. Finally it needed the glorious old hymn tunes and the majesty of their words to let it out. Dear land that I shall love, I'm glad to be British today."

On the last night at sea Scotty bought a bottle of champagne in the same spirit, the only way he knew to share with us his burst of excitement at the sight of the first lighthouse of home. After the toasts the Major dashed his glass into the hearth and we all followed suit. I have realized since that England was far from the responsible altruistic nation that I believed in at that time, and that the League of Nations and its successor, the United Nations, are only as honest and idealistic as the people in them. My love for England is clearer-eyed now, with a powerful element of irony in it, but it is still strong.

The trip handed us a bonus. We were due to dock in

London at dawn, but during the evening a fog closed in, and we woke to thick mist and the discovery that we had not even started our journey up the Thames. Reprieve!

"After lunch we suddenly were very thrilled to see the Major's training ship, the *Worcester*, and saluted it with ceremony. Then we went madly off to learn 'Here Come the British with a Bang – Bang' and sang it again and again, with gestures. Ships, ships, ships, freighters, barges, sailing smacks with red sails – the P&O [Pacific and Oriental Line], with stories of Shanghai in it, and all of us together and able to be very gay, gay to the last, when we went up to say goodbye to the captain. After kissing each of us heartily and talking to the men, he came down for an extra hand around and shot the ground from under us. Twenty-two transport ships left England today, he said, each carrying probably two thousand men, and the Major said quietly, 'That means that the balloon has gone up,' and we knew that he would be going too."

We were thrown into a numb sort of shock at the realization that when we left the ship we might never see him again. By the time we were disembarked and the luggage assembled it was a dark rainy night, matching our mood. "I might have been all right, except that suddenly Elinor Christie and Scotty said goodbye and shook me too much to give me a chance to recover. I knew I couldn't say anything at all without crying and I had to get into the taxi and just pray that it would start, and as it was the tears were pouring before it went. Dreadful to see the Major standing there smiling, and the smile harder to bear than anything else would have been."

It was still raining in the morning when we set off from our comic little "private hotel" in Bayswater. Comic and in quotation marks because it was so incredibly out of an Edwardian novel, probably by E. M. Forster.

"Tuesday, October 8: Still in Craven Hill Road but with a difference. It was a funny day. We woke from bad dreams with the grief only a little stilled, ate a silent and rather exhausted breakfast, and went out to find London streaming with rain. We sloshed across Kensington Gardens, thrilled to be there, even though still heavy-hearted, and finally found Exhibition Road and the Royal College of Art. One of the small things that said London to me was the sign for Litter, in beautiful Roman lettering, illuminated."

We had a tiresome wait at the registrar's office, and very little satisfaction at the end of it. The school was designed for students working towards a degree and short-term applicants were not welcome. We were asked to come back with our portfolios of work but given little hope of admission. We decided at that point to look for lodgings. One of my favourite Dickens stories was *A Tale of Two Cities* and I had dreamed of living, like the Manettes, in a "quiet square in Soho." After a shocked exploration of Soho, a stone's throw from Piccadilly Circus with its constant crowds, in the heart of the noisiest concentration of shoddy sex shops and cheap cafés, that dream dissipated, and we remembered the Major's advice and turned towards Chelsea.

This was better, a charming district near the Thames with King's Road running through the centre of it parallel to the river. We enjoyed the narrow streets off the main thoroughfare with their workmen's cottages converted into sophisticated townhouses, all polished brass and pastel stucco. In Jubilee Place, a mews behind King's

Road, we found what we were looking for. It was a fine
big front room over a chemist's shop, with a fireplace (gas
to be sure), day-beds, good walnut furniture, drapes and
accessories chosen with taste, even sterling-silver flat-
ware, and the look of character and personality that made
it seem like home immediately. Unfortunately, the rent
was a bit more than we could pay. After we had looked
further and seen the rooms in our price range, we agreed
that it would be cheaper in the long run to love our home,
and spend time there happily, than to need refuge from
it. On the same floor, also vacant, was a smaller room,
with a single day-bed, but with complete kitchen equipment, just right for George when he arrived the next
week. Our room had only a hot plate. The bathroom, a
few steps down on the landing at the end of the hall, was
to serve these two rooms and those of the tenant below
us.

George Keith-Beattie was one of Nory's students who
had ventured into her private life, calling diffidently at
the house, escorting her where he might, developing into
a "follower." So far that was all he was, but he was a nice
lad, close to her in age, and she was rather glad that he
was to be with us in England.

"Trailing wearily home after house-hunting, we decided to find a bus, and in the process of dashing to the
curb to catch one, I fell flat in the wet street, cracking
down on the same elbow I had hurt on the boat. By the
time Nory reached me from the centre of the road things
were beginning to go black – and I barely had time to
thrust my bag and map at her and say 'hold this.'" Poor
Nory! There I was, flat on my back in the gutter among
the wet yellow leaves, the water running around me, eyes

wide open and out cold. She thought I was dead, and was already cabling home in her mind. While she was still standing helpless with horror a policeman strode up and waved down a cruising London County Council ambulance. "It seemed funny to be wet in bed, and there was no time or place – it was all rather comfortable and damp and far away, and then suddenly there were Nory and a bobby and a strange man, all looking exceedingly worried, and I knew what had happened, and felt all shaken and weak and ashamed."

We were driven home to the hotel, and I was helped upstairs, feebly protesting, to the accompaniment of a lecture from the ambulance attendant on the folly of burning the candle at both ends. So we were in our little room, surrounded by wet clothes and underwear, all spread out to dry, Doris in bed and Nory hovering, when the Major was announced. From the depths we were raised to the very peak. Until that moment we had not been sure. Perhaps our friendship was just a shipboard game to him. And now we knew it was real to all of us.

"Bless him, bless him, bless him. He's still real. Nothing has happened yet. He's been to the War Office and apparently they have promised him the job he wants, but he's not being sent yet and he'll be here again Friday. He was tearing to the station to catch a train. I'm only afraid he may not have caught it, and we watched him off from the door, his black hat jammed on, his raincoat swinging, and us feeling like new people because of having seen him and touched him again."

14

The Iron Jelloids

WE RETURNED to the Royal College of Art laden with our portfolios but were advised that the Central School of Arts and Crafts was the place for us, being geared to advanced students who wanted specialized or short-term study. It was good advice. We were given a cordial welcome at the Central School and charmed by the principal, who allowed us to choose our own combinations of classes. Because of the mandate of the school it was obligatory to include one craft, so I signed up for bookbinding in the evening and Nory chose fashion drawing. Until the following week, when classes would begin, we were free to move into Jubilee Place, get settled, and explore London.

We did our exploring in widening circles, starting along King's Road with the butcher shop across the street. Jones Bros. Emporium, with its sawdust-covered floor and scrubbed wooden counters, was presided over

by two shaky old men in long white aprons. Nory dubbed
them the Jones boys, and we learned to appreciate the
privilege of buying as few as one or two eggs at a time.
We walked up and down the narrow streets that led off
King's Road, relishing the handsome stone facades with
their wrought-iron railings and shining brass door-plates
and the former workmen's cottages that had been renovated and turned into sophisticated townhouses. I located
Chelsea Old Church and promised myself to get to know
it. Chelsea is full of blue plaques proclaiming the great
men who lived in this house or that, Thomas Carlyle,
Ruskin, Sir Joshua Reynolds among others. We found
Henry VIII's old hunting lodge, now a nursery school.
From the embankment we watched the ebb tide leaving
boats stranded on the sloping muddy sides and saw the
river swift and shining in mid-stream.

As soon as we had tidied our luggage out of sight and
laid in some provisions we were ready for the Major. We
made tea for him and told him of our wanderings. We
were thrilled that he had worried about us, glad that he
liked our digs, proud that he approved of our address,
and interested to hear about his day at the War Office,
where a pompous desk-type had roused his ire. The war
scare seemed to be receding and this individual had
snubbed him rather than snapping him up for service.
Every prospect of delay cheered us. Scotty came for
supper minutes after the Major had left, full of his attempts to find a new job, and eager to talk about his wife
and little daughter who would be joining him as soon as
the job was firm. Nory read some of her poems to Scotty
and me, and their loveliness went to my soul with a new
shock of surprise. She had a rare gift of words. It was the

first time I had heard her read her own serious poetry, and the setting and occasion added to their appeal, lamplight on our blue pottery vase full of bronze mums, a big bowl of apples and grapes on the table, the first full evening we had been in our own home in London.

The next day we ventured as far as Kensington Gardens, already known to me from reading James Barrie. It was thick with prams and English nursemaids in grey or blue uniforms and caps with veils, children like leaves blowing about, as colourful and beautiful and restless. We agreed that it took a childhood of romping in parks to produce people like the Major. There were nice-looking Englishmen in trench coats striding along the paths with big dogs. As we came through the gardens the trees were high, leafy, and branching, dull in colour compared to Canada's; but the grass was a singing green.

The Central School of Arts and Crafts was several miles from Chelsea, close to Bloomsbury. We might have been wise to look for lodgings near the school, but both the number 19 and the number 22 buses stopped almost at our door and took us all the way, past endlessly interesting London sights. The commercial part of King's Road ended at fashionable Sloane Square, and the bus turned up Sloane Street of the smart dress shops and three-storey stone townhouses. Knightsbridge had Hyde Park on the left, with a glimpse of the riders in Rotten Row and of Park Lane at Hyde Park Corner, where we swung around the superb artillery memorial. Along Piccadilly we could peer into the windows of the gentlemen's clubs on the north side or look down on Green Park on our right and see where Constitution Hill led away towards Buckingham Palace and Pall Mall. At Piccadilly

Circus we circled the statue of Eros poised on one toe; we
had a tour of the theatre district along the edge of Soho
as the bus worked its way up Shaftesbury Avenue to High
Holborne, where the school stood at the corner of
Theobald's Road. It was a stone building dark with London grime, but full of bright hopes for us.

I had asked for a timetable that would concentrate on
drawing and painting. I was given four mornings working
from the nude model and two afternoons with a costumed
model. As well, I studied illustration with John Farleigh
and lettering with the great Edward Johnson and, best
of all, zoo drawing with John Skeaping. The other students seemed to be our age or slightly younger, the girls
with shrill, assured public-school voices, the men mind-
ing their own business. Nobody greeted us or showed the
slightest interest.

"Our first day at school seemed very short. We drew
hard all morning and all afternoon, with indifferent results, except for a very healthy backache. It seems strange
to be in that art school world without really feeling of it.
At the pub in Red Lion Square at lunch-time I listened to
the chatter in correct English around us and envied them
the accent that is theirs by pure accident rather than their
own efforts. It was fun to lean out of the window during
the model's rest and find ourselves looking down on the
jumbled chimney-pots and curving narrow streets of
London."

"Saturday: Much of today was made up of pinching
myself or squeezing Nory's arm to be sure that it's real.
It's been a day of rare deep joy that has been made up of
nothing but the gladness of being here. I left Nory ironing
this morning and went to Canada House by myself. The

first lions I saw from the bus said Trafalgar Square to me,
so off I hopped, and, thanks to the map, realized suddenly
that here I was at Westminster Abbey. I didn't go in,
keeping it for a ceremonial first visit, but I walked on
winged feet up Whitehall. It was part of the magic of the
day that I should pass just as the guard was being
changed. I stood on tiptoe peeping through the fence over
the top of the shoulders and was thrilled by the flashing
silver helmets, white-plumed, the scarlet tunics, resplendent with braid, and the swords, and more than all, with
the black lambskin fur saddle robes and the restless
horses."

Canada House touched me suddenly with unexpected
poignancy. I pored over the register, to be rewarded by
Mary Deeves of the Ontario Girls' Work Board,
Marjorie's cousin Esther MacWaters and her mother,
Mrs. R.Y. Eaton (one of *the* Eatons), Mr. and Mrs. Lismer
and their daughter Marjorie, and Ruth Home, whom I
knew through the Royal Ontario Museum. On the way
back I spent the lucky coin that Marjorie's brother Harry
had given me and bought a second-hand copy of *The Little
White Bird*, then on to spend the afternoon in Kensington
Gardens, sketching the children beside the Round Pond,
watching the afternoon die in a grey haze that came gently
down over the pond and the great spreading trees near
it. It felt perfect to be reading Barrie there, like something
long dreamed of, and suddenly true.

Once George had arrived our housekeeping settled
into a routine. Miss Busbridge, soon affectionately short-
ened to "the Buzz," was a sharp-nosed and sharp-voiced
landlady who soon taught us to leave the beds, the clean-

ing, and the breakfast dishes to her. Nobody else could meet her standard. For a week, we came home each day to find that she had also rearranged our groceries and dishes. After we had given up trying to maintain our own kind of order, she said to us, "I wondered how long it would take you to adapt yourselves to my better way of doing things." We stopped struggling and got along with her famously from then on.

A test of stamina was provided by the bathroom down the hall. It had no heat, and since it did have a gas heater to warm the bathwater, it had by law a permanently open window, which ensured that the temperature was at least as cold as out-of-doors. When you put your pennies in the slot of the gas heater you had a choice of a reasonable stream of warm water, which could not warm the cold bath or you, or a thin trickle of very hot water. I chose the latter, which gave me two inches of stinging heat to sit in and a fog of steam ascending to the ceiling, where it condensed, and from which it dripped in chilly drops onto my back while I scrubbed.

"Monday, October 14: Another day of drawing – with a gnawing ache in the back of the neck, and an amusing sense that the criticisms sound familiar. Haven't I heard those words before or even used them – not once but scores of times? It was a funny day in spots. Nory was late getting ready to leave and I was grumpy about losing my gloves, and I hurried us onto the wrong bus this morning, and the day passed with less than our usual sociability."

"Tonight the Major walked down to the embankment with us and we leaned on the stone wall, looking up and down the river, all dark blue and mysterious, with mist lying in ribbons, and a string of small boats tied together dark against the water near us."

"October 15: Our first lesson in book illustration today, with Nory hearing with secret amusement her own teaching points flung back to her in even her own words. I liked Mr. Farleigh, enjoyed his presentation of the problem, but we struggled over ideas and all we got for our pains was (a) hysterics, (b) one Bayer aspirin advertisement. First letter from M tonight, forwarded from Canada House, just a newsy bit of gossip really. She sounds busy and happy."

"October 16: Zoo all morning, with a fierce pain in the middle but with joy at the end of it. Mr. Skeaping gave us a lesson at the end of the morning that left both of us thrilled to the ears with the possibilities of it. His point of view is new to me and most stimulating. He showed us how to find a single line that would express the movement of the animal, and then how to develop the form of the animal around the movement line. This afternoon I slugged hard on a Roman alphabet in pencil, and the teacher said that I had done a lot of work in a short time. Even such slight praise made me feel marvellous, all coy and gratified and pink. After we were home Scotty blew in, up on top of the world because he'd just landed a good job. He was so pleased, and I was so pleased that he had come right to us to tell us about it, and he leaned back in the chair and beamed and talked about 'home tomorrow.' We had just had tea, and I had spilled the coffee over Nory and my bed and the floor, when George arrived in a great swither, and Scotty left before the tumult and the shouting had died."

"October 17: Yesterday Mr. Skeaping explained that outline was a vain hope, and solid form the only logical approach to drawing, and we bowed our heads and said 'aye.' Today the attractive-looking young woman in green advised me to spend more time on construction and to ignore shading. 'Let your line suggest the form.' Whom do I believe? No wonder the poor kids at CTS used to tear their hair."

"October 18: Very late. I was tired out tonight after school, but dinner was a specially gala affair, clean table-cloth, candlelight, and sherry – and we were all gay. For an hour or so after supper we worked hard and happily till the room began to get cold. Then, huddled over the fire in George's room, we started on budgets and discovered to our dismay that we were spending far more than we ought. It was a solemn evening from then on, with Nory cutting George down to two shillings per week for cigarettes and George not liking it much."

"Monday, October 21: Today was life drawing all day, with a marvellous model, a golden-brown boy who had a beautiful body, well-muscled and yet young and full of form, and reminding both Nory and me of Florida [Nory's sailor on the *American Farmer*]. Memorable also for a criticism from Mr. Farleigh that pepped me all up, simplicity of solid form, *selection* as the prime task of the artist. At noon Nory and I were full of vigour but it ebbed with the afternoon for my drawing then was just as dull, and less observant. Nory had a pain in her tummy, so that life looked a bit gloomy till supper, then off we went tonight to see *Top Hat* and laughed and laughed and laughed! We had to queue for half an hour. It was fun standing there on Haymarket, theatre lights behind and

before, watching a lad do acrobatics in the middle of the
street, and listening to desperately bad singing and even
worse guitar music. We were impervious to hats and tin
cups till one of the feeblest tenors rendered 'We May
Never Meet Again,' and then we broke down and parted
with a penny. As one of us said, 'If the fool had sung "Be
Still My Heart" [one of our songs from the *American
Farmer*] he might have had a shilling.'"

"October 24: I had fun today in costume class, a great
splashy water-colour this morning, and a Conté-and-
wash this afternoon of the old man in the medieval robe,
and I cleaned out my locker this morning and discovered
that after two weeks my life drawings don't look nearly
so bad as I remembered them being. On such trifles does
happiness depend."

"October 25: After being told by every instructor separately, *with* diagrams, I'm gradually beginning to believe
that my life drawings are lousy, over-worked, lacking
solidity and construction. The criticism today left me not
a leg to stand on. Everything was wrong, starting with
size, working right through action and proportion and
ending up with the modelling and detail. It's the most
discouraged I've felt yet, but by gum I'm going to learn
or bust."

"Monday, October 28: All day at school I simply
slugged, putting heart and soul into trying to simplify my
drawing, reduce it to the least common denominator, but
keep it right, solid and forceful. I was still sweating over
it this afternoon when the old boy with the game leg came
by and gave me a criticism that simply floored me! I
haven't ever before been so taken aback by a criticism:
(a) 'careless,' (b) 'photographic,' and he told me nicely

that I musn't expect to draw well after one lesson or even two or three. It took a long time to learn. He made a little allegory of the child learning to draw his alphabet slowly and carefully first, so that eventually he could write them right off. I felt so discouraged and so misjudged that I wept, and I spent the rest period leaning out of the window with Nory, furtively wiping up my tears with her rather smudgy handkerchief. If, after ten years, a man quite sincerely thought they were done by a beginner, what *is* the use?"

That was a bad day. We had dinner guests that night, friends of the Major's, and served steak that blew the budget for the whole week.

We were due to spend the weekend in the Balbernie ménage, at Beaconsfield, a village an hour or so from London, and anticipated our visit in a fine state of eagerness and nerves. We wanted to see the Major in his own setting and meet his family, but we were afraid his wife, Doris, would resent our devotion to her husband and the attentions he was paying us. Nory was fighting flu, and I collapsed with it as soon as we returned, in spite of which we looked back on the weekend with pleasure. Doris Balbernie had given us a warm welcome although we looked in vain for any of the shared fun that was so constant an element in our friendship with the Major.

"Both the children are darlings, Barry's smile goes all over, from blue eyes to wide mouth. It is his main social weapon. Richard smiles less, perhaps because he's older, but he is very companionable. I liked the Major's remark to him when we were out in the woods sketching: 'If you fall and break your neck, will you remember to tell your mother that I strictly forbade you to climb that tree?'"

After sketching, we walked on to the Royal Standard, said to be the second-oldest pub in England, and if the day before had seemed unreal, this seemed quite fantastic, all the elements of an English three-act farce set up, one half-timbered inn front, one garden set with tables and chairs, one fence and hedge in front, all complete with Englishmen in plus-fours and pipes and bright young things with clipped English voices, the side garden with apple trees, benches, and old stone sculptures with the noses chipped off.

"Jubilee Place, November 9: Eight youths singing 'Good night, baby, Good night, milkman's on his way!' outside the window. Cold inside, the kettle slowly heating for our hot-water bottles, canvases on the 'blackened' hearth, presumably drying. George and Nory working in moody silence next door, where the gas has failed. We spent the afternoon at the exhibition of the London Group, a sufficiently interesting show but, to George at least, deeply distressing. I rather enjoyed it, and I was even thrilled to discover that three of the things at which I exclaimed with genuine enthusiasm were by Mr. Farleigh and Mr. Porter. Porter paints in a way of which I thoroughly approve, and, seeing that he will be teaching me painting, that pleased me. Yesterday Nory and I went downstairs to see the painting class and found an elegant nude model, a roly-poly Negress, which thrilled us sufficiently to send us all over London, down streets with entrancing names and through crowded ways, after canvas and stretchers. Last night I wrestled with them all evening and fell into bed weary and disgruntled."

The flu had used up our energy. And the dark days of autumn, with fog and cold that clutched at ankles and crept up through our clothes, kept us debilitated. We worked all together in George's room because we could keep feeding shillings to the gas fire and huddle over it for warmth. The Buzz would come in and gasp at the heat, assuring us that we were in dire need of fresh air! We were certainly in need of something.

The bright spot was our introduction to the Major's American friends, Ted and Elizabeth Acheson, young, sophisticated, travelled, and prepared to keep an eye on us for his sake. They lived in one of the charming renovated old houses that gave Chelsea its character. And Daphne and Gunther lived with them, two schnauzers, who, while obviously dogs, shared so many of the Achesons' social graces that they seemed more like people. Daphne spoke French, and Gunther English, with or without an American accent, and they knew by the language used which of them was being addressed. Perhaps it was Elizabeth who reminded us that we probably needed sunshine and advised us to get ourselves some vitamins as a substitute. It was amusing and rather nice to hear her slow southern accent and her American turns of phrase. Elizabeth, with her blonde hair and perfectly tailored grace, looked as if sunshine followed her about. Ted was fair too, with short hair that wanted to kink, and a careless loose-limbed look that made me think of the deck of a sailboat. He was in England to work on a book and because he loved the country.

When he needed a break from his typewriter on a Saturday he would occasionally phone and suggest an outing to Battersea Park, and we would all troop over there to give the dogs a run and feed the gulls. Ted was full of nonsense such as offering the gulls indigestion tablets along with the brick-hard crusts he was throwing them. The Achesons gave us a welcome chance to do something for them when they let us paint murals on their dining-room walls. And they did something special for us when they included us in the party to celebrate the publication of John Gunther's *Inside Europe*. Ted's brother was Dean Acheson, secretary of state in Washington. We listened that night to Gunther and Ted swapping stories about the great on two continents.

The Achesons nicknamed us the Iron Jelloids in compliment to the sign that hung out under our window above the chemist shop. We might have been well advised to try the jelloids to counteract the London damp and cold.

"November 10: Tonight I did some Conté scribbles of George's room, the window with the washing hanging in front of it, the litter on the table, and the stove corner. They were fun to do, and, like most drawings done for fun, look better than the laboured ones."

"November 11: Armistice Day. Nory and I were at Whitehall by 9:15 and already the crowd was piled up along the sidewalks. We joined it, and had an amusing hour watching bobbies make walls of themselves, seeing the guardsmen come by in their enormous busbies, with a carriage of such extravagant arrogance that we hugged ourselves in delight. They were beautiful to watch, arms swinging, shoulders high, chests fully out and their whole march a swagger. The air force lined up right in front of us with a precision that was alarming but explained by the hatchet face of the officer in charge. They moved as one man, their rifles striking the ground with a single clap, and the perspiration dripping down their callow faces and into their collars. The sun came out palely at first, and

then more strongly, and the day was beautiful, and just
down the street the tower of Big Ben was a pale grey
shape in the sky, and the buildings even directly opposite
were hazy too. Then the music began with the tones as
rich and vibrant as a symphony orchestra, the pipers high,
shrill, and piercing, yet terribly beautiful. I wish I had
known the words to 'Flowers of the Forest.' I wondered
if the Major was anywhere within earshot. Chopin's
Funeral March was the one I loved best, and 'God Save
the King.' Then Big Ben chimed, the gun fired, and into
a deepening silence came the eleven heavy booms of Big
Ben. When it had finished the hush settled down like a
physical presence over the crowd. I heard a rushing,
rustling rattle, and looked up to find that it was the leaves
of a little plane tree nearby. That somehow said more than
anything, that the silence should be so complete that it let
the leaves speak, probably the only time in the whole year
when one could hear them in London."

"November 20: We started painting today, and everything looked all right till I began putting body colour on.
Then, as usual, all the vitality of my turps wash vanished."

"November 24: Went to Tottenham Corner to see
Mickey and Kitty and had a grand visit with them. Mick
had so much to get off his chest and we walked around
Epsom Downs for a while. The new baby is a sweet little
thing. I do like Kitty and my heart aches for the disap-
pointments and worries they have had."

Mickey and Kitty Jillings were an English couple who
had lived next door to us on Balsam Avenue before
returning to England. Mickey was tense and jittery,
struggling back from a nervous breakdown that had left
him in a deep depression. He was utterly exasperated by

what he considered English business conservatism and stupidity, most of which he blamed on the entrenched class system. Kitty suggested that I let Mick show me some of the England that he still loved. "It will do him good."

"December 3: Started terribly early with a dash to dress and meet Mickey at the coach station, and then we were off for the day, a grand day in many ways. The sun shone till afternoon, not bad for an English sun, and, after we had passed all the suburbs, we came through English countryside, the trees mossy and ivy-twined, the hayricks top-heavy and thatched, and some marvellous old 'beamy' houses, as Mickey would put it. Bits I liked best were the Georgian house where Burne-Jones lived, and the three flint houses in Rottingdean, the one with the smugglers' cave, and all the tiled roofs and little gables. And the champagne! And the walk up over the downs with the sherry and beer and sea-mist lending the place a rather dreamy quality. Tea was in front of the fire, with the sea outside, and then there was the little moment down beside the breakers. Poor lad. I do ache for him. He's pulling up a long tough road. He's still as erratic and jumpy as he could be." This was the first of many dates that Mickey made with me, either in London or off by bus to a park or village beyond.

"December 5: Farleigh said today that I was almost too slick in my water-colour – I needed to think more of the drawing, but with my gratefulness for crumbs I was able to feel bucked that he said I handled water-colour re-markably well. 'Perhaps it's just instinctive with you.' Yesterday at the zoo Mr. Skeaping said to forget tech-nique for a bit and begin to draw your thoughts. I remem-

bered Lismer's 'Think a think and draw a line around it.'
I feel as if I hadn't heard it or thought it since first year
at OCA. It's the thing I need drilled into me most."

"Sunday, December 8: It was fine when I propped
open the first eye this morning, so I dressed in haste and
made for Hampstead. When I came out of the under-
ground the air seemed clearer, the sky brighter, and the
country higher than in Chelsea. And up at the top of the
hill, just before the little pond where the children were
sailing their boats, was my first ever Punch and Judy
show, and I leapt to it, thrilled that my blighted youth
should know fulfilment at this late date. It was grand fun.
When Punch and the man were chasing each other and
Punch kept popping out of the side or the back or anywhere except where the man was, the children jumped
and shrieked in excitement. 'There he is! There he is!'
And then when he cracked Punch over the head and
turned to tell the children he was dead, they screamed at
him, 'He moved. He's alive. There he is!' I was almost
shrieking with them. They were lovely children, rosy-
cheeked, vital – and their mummies and daddies and
nurses were so amused that the whole group felt very
friendly. I walked away on air."

"December 13: I have enjoyed painting today, less
because the results are good than because I appreciate so
much Mr. Porter – both himself and his attitude to us, and
what he is teaching us. Thank heavens I'm happy about
the painting. It's the most important of all to me."

For Nory and me, one of the pleasures of London was
George's enjoyment of it. At Kensington Gardens, I reported, "George was such fun. It was worse than the toy
shop. First of all we lost him to the kites, and he stood

with his hands in his overcoat pockets, bare-headed,
oblivious to all but the small boys reeling them in or
letting them unwind as the wind took them up and up and
up and up, some so high they were hard to find, and the
string soon vanished into air so that they seemed to be
floating of themselves. I wonder how long the boys have
been saving cord from parcels. Around the pond it was
the sailboats that fascinated George while we loved best
the people and the gulls, their tails brilliantly white, their
wings almost blue against the grey water and the greyer
trees and buildings behind the pond. One old man sat on
a bench, a dumpy shape with two brown-and-white pup-
pies in his coat, just their inquisitive heads peeking out.
There were many fair-haired, fair-cheeked children with
brimmed sailor hats, gloved hands, and long legs under
their tailored coats, and a few couples, one frankly em-
bracing. We left George staring at a motorboat, and
decided to let him catch us, but when we had reached
almost the end of the park, and he was still glued to the
side of the bench where the owner was tinkering with it,
and the crowd grew and faded and grew and faded, but
still George stuck, we walked back to get the housekey.
George looked at us blankly, then came slowly recognition, and he returned in layers from some happy world
known only to small boys and their ilk. Dear Round
Pond, dear Kensington. 'The pleasantest club in London'
surely."

"1935, Christmas in London: I've never in my life
before known a Christmas of such quality. Even the alarm
clock had a bell sound this morning. Even the first groggy
half-hour was a Merry-Christmas one. There were the

bulging stockings pushed aside so that the fire might be lit, and the tree dark, but with silver sparkling in little bright points from the fire."

Elinor Christie from the *American Farmer* came to stay on Christmas Eve, which we spent in front of the fire reading Dickens's *A Christmas Carol* aloud, and she was with us for the morning festivities of breakfast and parcels. Presents were few, and strictly budgeted, but carefully chosen. Nory and George had gone together to buy me *Moby Dick*, with the Rockwell Kent illustrations, still treasured for itself and the memories it conjures. We had bought George a tin flute capable of real tunes, and Nory had gone all out to buy him a top hat. We had an album of *American Farmer* snapshots for Elinor.

As we left the house with our presents for the Balbernies, George carrying a bowl of goldfish, Nory with an offering of champagne for the Major, Doris with a bag full of oddments, the bathroom window on the second floor was flung open and Miss Busbridge's head, in its wild morning frenzy, popped out. "Get a day return ticket!" abruptly, above the bells. All the way up Jubilee Place we heard the chimes, nearer, farther, soft and confused, clearer. The air was distantly full of them and the clouds were bright and broken to let blue sky through. The goldfish splashed, George dripped, and we laughed.

Gathered at Beaconsfield when we arrived, besides the Balbernie family whom we had met in November, there was Mrs. Wheeler, the Major's mother, an alert greyhaired woman who ran her late husband's importing business in the City, and Kitty, his sister, who shared our adoration of Arthur and embraced us as kindred souls.

"The room was hung with great red and green gar-
lands, the table literally hidden under pyramids of Christmas crackers, blue, red, green, gold, silver, cellophane
and patterned, with Mrs. Balbernie sending Nory and me
down beside the Major, which made us happier than the
mere joy of being near him because it was a gesture of
sympathy and generosity. And besides grand turkey there
was champagne and a toast to the two dears, Major and
Mrs. B., and such a pulling of crackers as I have never
seen before, dozens for each. Then the pudding, with a
great thick cluster of holly in it, and blue flames leaping
around it, and such things inside. A wedding ring first for
the Major. 'Doris,' says he to his wife, 'it's true.' And then,
oh horrors, a thimble for me, symbol of spinsterhood,
which I quickly covered up again with pudding and gave
a loud moan. After the commiseration had subsided I
prepared for the worst and dived for it, and found a
handle on top, which made it a *bell*. Could anything be
more fitting or auspicious than an apparent thimble
which turns out as a bell?"

We listened together to the Empire Broadcast, on radio
of course. "The best fun was that every solitary person
who spoke in any of the ten centres seemed to have
relations in Canada, and sent greetings to Aunt Ella and
Uncle Willie and the cousins. It became quite absurd.
Our whole ten millions must be cousins or aunts or
uncles. The King sounded distressingly husky, as if each
word was an effort, either physically or emotionally, and
then we stood at attention while 'God Save the King' was
sung, and I watched the flame of the fire and followed the
voices from England to Scotland to Wales to Ireland, and
we sat down, still thinking of Mother and Grandfather

listening at home, Marjorie and Roy, the Beers, all the hosts of them."

Mrs. Wheeler asked us at one point in the afternoon if we three all came from the same village. Suddenly we realized how blank was her picture of Canada. I explained that we all came from the same *place*, but that it was a large city, seven miles from home to work. "How do you get there?" And I found myself telling her that I paddled along the lake past the Indian encampments to reach Central Technical School, and Nory assured her that the wolves hardly ever came down Yonge Street. Kitty swallowed the story of the side-hill gouger from snout to tail and commented, "Do you know, the more I hear about Canada, the more fascinating I think it is."

Early in January I took off for a weekend in Paris with Kathleen Hilken, an English girl who had been with me at the Ontario College of Art and now lived in London. We walked miles in and out of the galleries, cramming that precious weekend full, and managing to include even the Folies Bergères, which in those days depended on music and dancing as well as on nakedness. "The moment we had fought our way in the door we were captured by the gaiety of the theatre. The entrance was a huge café with housefronts on all sides, awnings, a great wide staircase, tables, and a bar. The show itself moved with colourful music and fun all through. I adored the naked dancers. They had all the allure possible and still were artistic instead of vulgar. The girls were beautiful, superb figures, all pink and white and blooming in the strong lights, their hair uniformly golden, feet beautiful, lovely breasts and hips. They were delights to look at – and sexy! No matter what the scene, what the costumes, it was beautiful."

It was the memory of that show that took me back to the Folies fifteen years later, when I was in Paris with Nory's successor at Central Tech, Virginia Luz. This time it was a disaster, no talent, no imagination, only naked-ness and ostrich feathers. I wrote that it was "a terrific fuss over nothing, and we walked out at intermission, glad to come home to bed."

Back to London and hard work at school. "January 18: The King is ill. The wireless news was not particularly reassuring, and we saw a man's paper on the bus tonight saying that his heart was a little weaker. It seems possible that it is the end. It's strange to think of it and to realize how deeply affectionate and concerned everyone in Lon-don and England and the Empire feels. King George is so much more than a symbol. The prince must dread his death, from every point of view. Kipling died early this morning, and the newspaper memoirs of his life and writings have been reminding me of how much more he was than just a British jingoist."

Three days later King George V died. The bulletins had hardly appeared on the boards before every shop on our bus route to the Central School – Sloane Street, Knightsbridge, and Piccadilly – was stripped of colour and draped entirely in black and purple. I left school for Temple Bar to see and hear Edward VIII proclaimed king.

"I went in the general direction as fast as I could walk, and found myself following others through Lincoln Fields Inn to Bell Yard Road where it joins Fleet Street.

There I stayed, jammed into a crowd, and grateful for the little mirror that let me see quite decently into the centre of the street. Without it, all I could see in front of me was bowler hats. It was a very sober crowd. Heaps of the men were in black ties. All the women on the balconies of the buildings opposite were in black, and the city has worn a subdued air that is the result of real affection and sincere grief. There was no badinage and little conversation in the crowd. It was difficult to see, but there was much arriving of betasselled coaches with coachmen in silk hats and beautiful men in red uniforms with great cascades of white feathers in the helmet, and the Horse Guards resplendent in shining silver and red and white, and heralds in little gold caps, gold tunics with braid right across their tummies, blowing a flourish of trumpets on long silver horns. I could see the judges or whoever they were, in white silk wigs and dark robes. And I could hear someone calling a loud challenge, 'Who's there?' to the procession as it approached the boundary of the old City. Then it passed, and in a few minutes, far away and hard to understand, after another double flourish of trumpets, came the proclamation itself. I could distinctly hear his name, 'Edward – Albert – Christian – George – Andrew – Patrick – David.' I thought of Marjorie and the way we used to string off those names. And then there was cheering and 'God Save the King,' played very slowly, and with people singing softly but in such numbers that it sounded like the moaning of wind, all around, deep and very powerful."

The next day I stayed at an upstairs corner window of the school to watch the cortège on its way from King's

Cross station to the lying in state in St. Paul's Cathedral.
High Holborne was kept clear by a wall of bobbies, but
the side-streets were dense with people.

"It was a dark crowd, in black, and a very quiet one.
The procession came in silence, half a dozen mounted
men, a line of mounts drawing the gun carriage and the
bier, which was covered with the gold flag and its red lion,
topped by a small crown and a single cross of flowers.
That was all. Behind it came the prince, King Edward
VIII, walking in a distressed sort of way as if his feet hurt,
and beside him Lord Harewood and the Duke of York.
After them, the cabinet, bare-headed, dressed in black
and very quiet, followed by some more guards."

"February 14: A cable from Marjorie today: 'Kindling
delivered September' – and I'm so glad for her. I had to
walk right out and send a cable back and nothing I could
think of sounded pleased enough. I'm glad I'll be home
before the baby comes and I keep wondering why I'm so
sure it's to be a girl. I never think of girls – and yet this
time I do.

"Today Mr. Porter introduced me to his way of doing
water-colours, a new way to me, leaving all your lights
white and modelling the rest in a high key, with a brush
that's practically dry."

"February 17: Yesterday we had a new pose and I
plunged into it, full of confidence and determination to
use all the things Mr. Porter had taught me. I slapped the
paint on and had a grand time. And he said 'good,' and,
better than that, *I* said 'good.' I went down to look at it
today and it's still good! That makes it worth all the
sweating and cursing I've done to date. If only I can keep
the vitality and freshness when I work further into it. I

had the best time yesterday. I wish it were always first day at a pose."

Spring in England was a revelation to me. The whole earth seems to open out and burst into bloom. And it wasn't just the crocuses. March came with birdsong and sunshine and found me capitulating to Mickey's need of me, to the flattery of his attentions, and the sweetness of being in love in London in the spring. Kitty sent us here and there with her blessing, eventually for an idyllic few days together on the Isle of Wight, where we walked hand in hand on the chalk downs, high above the sea; later we went for a full week to the Isle of Man. My memories of those months are grateful, full of tenderness and pain, knowing always that this was for now, and not for the rest of my life. Mickey rationalized our "affair" as good for me, because it enlarged my experience as a woman and therefore as an artist. I rationalized it as good for both Kitty and Mick because it brought him out of a long period of apathy and depression, which had threatened their marriage more than I did. Nory and I talked it out, and she forgave me, the more easily that she was still carrying in her heart the girlhood idol with whom she had been travelling when he was arrested, and who was still serving a term for bank robbery in America. The Major and the Achesons raised no eyebrows and kept their thoughts to themselves, perhaps understanding my need better than I did myself.

"We sat on the sea-wall tonight and watched the exquisite silver thread of the moon in the sky and the faint glow of warmth at the horizon. A sky like a Japanese

print was reflected in the pools left by the tide. Thank
God Mickey can *see* things. We were walking very slowly
down the shore when suddenly he stopped and said, 'My
God,' or the equivalent, in a stricken kind of voice, and I
stopped short, stricken in turn and wondering what was
the matter. It was specially sweet to find that it was the
sheer beauty of the cliff and lights and rooftops at the end
that had stopped him." I told Mickey that night that I
should never see the thread of a new moon without
thinking of him, and I never have.

"March 21: This morning Nory and George and I
walked up to Hyde Park and through it in search of
spring, and it was there: crocuses in thick clusters around
the trees, people sculling on the Serpentine, and the three
of us lying on the grass in the sun, with lacy English
branches against a pale blue sky, and Nory and I ac-
knowledging homesickness for our dear north country.
This morning I felt what exile could be, how I would cry
with longing for the feel of a paddle in my hand, the
warmth of flat Georgian Bay rocks, the cool ripple of blue
water. And then I came home to a huge sheaf of iris, and
my heart sang inside me. I see them last thing at night and
first thing in the morning."

"May 5: Nory and I cut wood blocks and played a game
this afternoon called 'What are the six best things in life?'
I had read her the article from the *Express* this morning,
and in the bus by myself I had decided that the two very
best were walking in the woods, and being loved, in that
order. I think even life without love would be better than
life without quietness and beauty out of doors. Nory still
puts dancing with Ron at the top. I wonder how much of
her heart he still has."

Kitty and Mickey and their two children were all moving back to Canada in the summer, to settle in Vancouver. I joined them for a few days before they went, for a long weekend playing with small Robin on the seashore, walking all together on the Downs, picnicking among gorse bushes, and being, astonishingly, comfortable together. Kitty was warm and relaxed. I admired her and liked her immensely. That made it easier to say goodbye to them, with my pain at parting from Mick a small price to pay for what they had given me.

"Sunday, May 24: A day that I am glad to have lived. We went to Kew on faith, complete with sandwiches, and found ourselves in a world that was too beautiful to be borne. The laburnum everywhere, a cold green yellow as a singing relief to the masses of pinks and purples of the rhododendron. They were beyond description, beyond belief, and beyond remembrance. We were drunk on them. And I thought about it being Victoria Day at home, and perhaps my children's CGIT camp, and about Marjorie's letter, understanding about Mickey and not scolding me, and I thought too that only the steady pain of missing him kept me from being perfectly happy, and I wondered if I should miss the pain if it should ever go."

"May 27: At the zoo this morning I was drawing polar bears for the Major, and one of my gloves fell into the den and was gnawed by a large and dirty polar bear who pulled the fingers till they snapped back, lots of fun! But my life drawing today touched a new low, and I would be in complete despair except for Mr. Tomlinson's kind word of encouragement that a real low precedes a jump. Pray that the jump may come soon!"

"June 10: Only two more days left, and I didn't do a

single decent scratch today. But I had a good afternoon. Mr. Grant took me down to the library for a course on Degas and a talk for the good of my soul. He said that being this good I should be much better, that my drawings were worse than bad because they are mediocre, that I need more sensitive perception. My hand is okay, it's my eyes and brain that are failing. He told me to use charcoal for a while, to have some fun, to do bad drawings if it turned out so, to *feel* more."

"June 24: Today at the zoo began well in front of the chimps, in the big open cage, then in the Fellows' Garden with Mr. Skeaping ('John' since noon) sitting in a deck chair, glowing in the sunlight, and talking Life and Art, about the need of emotional and mental self-realization. I told him I felt a need for greater growth before I would have anything to say, and he said that people whose lives had been explosive were more readily able to express their personalities in their work. We looked across the green, level grass to the two camels, startling in the sunlight, with a multicoloured procession of children passing in front of them, and talked of the importance of seeing things as if for the first time, freshly.

"Later, I sat by myself in front of the polar-bear cage and reviewed the many different ways in which my teachers had given me the same verdict, remembering that Miss Dafoe had explained my poor mark in history in Fifth Form by my youth, and remembering my feeling then that there was very little I could do about that. Perhaps life will do it for me eventually. My part will be to say 'yes' to life."

15

Home Again

WE BOUGHT A CAR, a red Humber, for one hundred
dollars. It's hard to believe. For six weeks we explored
England and Scotland, using H.V. Morton's *In Search of
Britain* as our bible along the way, our only mechanical
trouble a windshield-wiper blade that needed replacement. Our passage home was booked on a ship that left
from Manchester, and, the day before we embarked,
George negotiated the sale of the car for seventy-five
dollars.

Our ship was another freighter, but carried only ten
passengers and with very little deck space. The tiny
lounge doubled as the dining room. One of our fellow
passengers was Helen Crichton – Crichty, as we called
her – head of the domestic art department at Central
Tech, whom we already knew well and liked. Another
was Barker Fairley, who was on his way to take over the
German department at the University of Toronto, with

his wife and teen-aged children. Barker was already
interested in art but had not yet begun his second career
as a distinguished Canadian painter. The company was
congenial but provided none of the high drama and
excitement of our passage to England. "Monotonous days
at sea" was my description of our voyage, until the pattern
was broken one memorable morning by the sight of land,
icebergs, porpoises, and whales.

"As soon as I went out on deck it was different. There
was a Cunarder near us, and I leaned over the rail and
watched her and counted her decks enviously, then went
aft with Mr. Fairley and talked Georgian Bay and paddling, hungrily, till a sailor laddie ran up and rang the bell,
saying, 'Iceberg off the port bow.' We tore to see it and
watched it grow from a light speck to a lovely fairy
creation of white and green shadows. We were still at
breakfast when someone shouted 'Land,' and we ran up
the corridor and out all the doors at once, and passed the
binoculars from one to another and shook hands on it,
and were very gay. And while we were still congratulating
each other on seeing land, someone noticed porpoises
popping in and out of the water too quickly for me to see
anything but the splashes. And then someone called out
'Whales,' and there on the other side of the ship, port, was
a whole school of them, lazily showing their great dark
slippery bodies with the pointed tails, and blowing and
spouting.

"And lastly there was Newfoundland, an irregular low
blue shape in the distance. And it's sunny! And the ship
has stopped heaving! And the Fairley family have recov-
ered! And I'm going *home*. I haven't dared to think about
it too much. Since Sunday we have had day after day

much the same, strong headwinds the whole time, the ship pitching and tossing, pitching and tossing, hours on the deck wrapped up tight but cold in spite of it, reading, watching the waves rolling past, grey or green or blue or black, dozing perhaps, thinking long hours about whether Mickey will meet me in Montreal and deciding no, playing bridge in the cabin and going to bed at 9:30. I can't believe two passages could be so different."

That night we finished the second bottle of the Major's farewell gift of wine, with much ceremony. Then we put into each bottle a letter to him, wrapped in a request that the finder use the enclosed ten cents to mail it. We dropped them gently into the sea, and eventually both letters reached him in England.

When we docked in Montreal Mother was there to meet me with Ken, who had come up from the States specially to drive her down. Mickey was there too, which just seemed to complicate life. We couldn't talk. Mother acknowledged him coolly. In a few meaningless minutes we had greeted and parted, with Ken bearing Nory and George and Mother and me off to Uncle Charlie's for dinner.

Toronto meant Marjorie, who had come in from Brampton to welcome me, very pregnant, very happy, and being everything that it meant to me to be home. She stayed with me that night, and we slept, as we had so often slept through the years, wrapped in each other's arms.

My CGIT group had set up a camp for the Labour Day weekend, a dramatic demonstration of their maturity, to which I was admitted without having to take any responsibility. I was still too disoriented to feel part of it.

"September 13: It's a year ago today that we left, and

I'm almost as unhappy now as I was happy then. Mother seems very miserable. She was fine in Montreal when she met me, all right while Ken was here. At first I thought she was tired, then I thought she was cross at me for having gone to camp. Now I don't know what it is, and I wish I could do something to help her."

The "kindling" was safely delivered, and for a short time Marjorie stayed at her mother's. "October 3: I went down the hill this morning and landed in the Beer household in a state of chaos, Mrs. B. in curlers, Marjorie in pyjamas, Harry [her brother] in pyjamas, Anne Eleanor in tears because she was hungry, so I bathed her, and watched her fed, and gossiped a bit and then home."

In many ways it was a grim autumn. Mother was silent or curt. Grandfather and Grace were affected by her ill humour, although we three were comfortable together. But the news of the world was bad. "Jim Hunter [newscaster] reporting on the war in Spain, Mully [at CTS] prophesying fascism in U.S., Quebec talking secession, Edward's abdication."

Eventually, in desperation, I broke into Mother's silence and discovered the reason for it. The weekend that I had been at camp with my Shawnees, Mother had dipped into my diary and discovered the whole horrible truth about Mickey and me. She had been devastated, to the point of taking her prayer book up to Dad's grave in Mount Pleasant Cemetery and reading the burial service for me as for one dead. For three months her anger had been fermenting, and the explosion was violent.

"January 1, 1937: Something has gone out of writing in my diary, perhaps for ever. After the first ghastly horror of my Christmas Eve talk with Mother, when her hysterical grief was so much worse and more bitter even than I had feared, God what hell Christmas was this year. From time to time since, in with the sick ache of pity for Mother and worry for the future, there has been a feeling of shame and outrage that *anyone* should have read my diary. It was a damnable trick – worse than peeking through keyholes. Nobody but God has any right to a person's inmost thoughts."

After Christmas I escaped to Haliburton, but my heartache went with me and I could not get Mother out of my mind. "I think if she knew how miserable and how helpless I feel, she might be a little revenged. If only she could once know what someone else feels about something. And I suppose she never will. She could even read my diary without understanding it. How it stings to think of her distorting everything she reads. Sometimes I could almost hate her for having read it, but mostly I feel too sorry for her and she is terribly important to me."

Ken wrote to me from Toledo, "I don't know or care what you have done, had a baby or married a foreigner, but you should never write anything down that you are not prepared to hear read out in court." Feeling too late the force of his ironic advice, I mutilated my journal, cutting away whole sections, and erasing every incriminating passage in which I had used Mickey's name.

Unable to help Mother myself, I told Dr. Cotton the story and asked him to talk to her. "January 7: I spent the last hour this afternoon in Dr. Cotton's office, and I feel now as if there were another strong hand in mine. He was kind and quiet and understanding and so sane. He and Ken have helped me back to a little sense of balance that I much needed."

For Mother, however, Dr. Cotton's visit was the last straw. My guilt was now known, and she could never hold up her head in public again!

A week later Grace and Grandfather and I stood on the platform of Union Station and saw the train pull out, taking Mother and her friend Mrs. Young off to Florida for a break that we all needed badly. We watched it disappear down the track and then looked at each other, the smiles spreading.

"Let's go to a movie," said Grandpa. I've forgotten what we saw, but I have never forgotten the three of us sitting around the kitchen table after midnight because nobody was sending us to bed, having a festive snack and a leisurely gossip. Grace had decided to stay the night because it was such a special occasion.

"Let me see," said Grandpa a few days later. "Tomorrow is Tuesday, and the next day is Wednesday, and on Thursday your mother will have been away a week, and the next Thursday it will be two weeks, and the Thursday after that, three weeks. How time flies!" Far too quickly for us.

I looked back on those weeks as a holiday. "And on one of our many nights at home together, in the corner of the living room, reading detective stories and trying not to hear the radio, Grandfather got to his feet and coughed, and said that he was going down to look at the furnace, 'in case I might miss him if he went out without saying goodbye.' He is such a dear."

Grace went up to town with him one day when he needed new shoes. Grace loved that. She was proud of being seen with this distinguished-looking old gentleman. But she didn't know which way to look when the clerk in

Eaton's shoe department asked what he was looking for, and Grandfather said with a twinkle, "They must be comfortable for dancing, and they must please her."

His eighty-fifth birthday fell during Mother's absence. We told him that Cousin Florrie was coming down for afternoon tea so he spruced himself up for the occasion. She was a part of the Lévis connection, a niece of whom he was very fond. Towards the end of the afternoon he whispered to me to ask Grace if it would be all right to invite her to stay for dinner. "Yes, indeed." And the Jenkings and Mrs. McGill arrived together shortly afterwards, to his surprise and delight. They were friends of Mother's whom he knew best and who loved Grandpa and enjoyed being with him.

"We all got terribly hilarious and the cake was perfect, a circle of candles and Happy Eighty-Fifth Birthday on it, and a rose in his buttonhole, and cocktails and beer and a general air of festivity."

Florida and Mrs. Young had been good for Mother. She came home refreshed, comparatively civil to me, and wanting to send us off for a holiday as soon as school was over. So Grandfather had the satisfaction of showing off Montreal and Quebec to the fresh and appreciative delight of Grace, who had never travelled before.

Early in July 1937 I left for my first experience of the west. Marjorie's sister, Eleanor, could not join me until later, but we planned to meet in Jasper and go on together. Depression travel was primitive but cheap. I went "colonist" in a car with black leatherette seats that made up into berths at night, and a stove at one end for preparation of food. Usually I bought a good breakfast in the dining car, still gracious with linen tablecloths and finger bowls. My other two meals were sandwiches bought in haste at station counters.

My goal was the YMCA camp near Jasper, where I was to wait for Eleanor and do some mountain painting. The camp was on Lake Edith, not far from Jasper Lodge, which I visited once to observe its elegance and luxury. The Y camp lacked these, but it had a wooden central dining hall and kitchen, and wooden floors under the canvas sleeping tents, which stood in a picturesque row facing the lake. The first morning I wakened to see a bear looking in the opening of the tent-flap. I froze but decided that, if he was on the loose, he was tame. He ambled off and left me free to dress.

Not so tame, I discovered. "Yesterday most of the campers went motoring, leaving just Briant, Don, and me in camp. We were sitting at our simple midday meal when we heard a few irregular noises outside, a growl and a shout. We three laid down our forks and knives without a word, pushed back our chairs and dashed to the window where we saw Max, the stout cook, half-way up the roof of the cook-house, and a huge brown bear and her cubs tearing at some big bones of raw meat. It was pretty exciting for a bit."

A few days after our arrival, six of us went by car, small boat, and a twelve-mile hike through the woods to Maligne Lake, to stay overnight in the tent hostel there. That evening the warden of the park invited me to his cabin to meet his wife, who was a painter and starved for someone to share it with. He took me by small motor boat to their house about a mile along the shore. I let the others go back to Jasper without me and had them send up my sketching gear with the next party, while I moved in with Charlie and Mona Matheson and small Glenn. What an experience: two weeks learning to know the lake and the mountains that circle it with people who belonged in that world and loved it.

The Mathesons came out with me when it was time to return to camp. We travelled by horse train, another wonderful first for me. That night I wrote, "I crawled into bed, and, just as I hit, suddenly it hurt. The soreness took me right back into this morning, three golden hours on the trail riding down from Maligne with a swinging movement that sometimes was almost like dancing, and the sun hot on my back, Mona and Charlie ahead on Saucy and Pilot with old black Mrs. Snaith trudging along and the bad brown Friendly stopping to graze, or turning aside, or biting Mrs. Snaith's rump until Charlie broke off a gad or slapped his rear end with his reins. And away at the back, almost too happy to bear it, came Doris on White Cloud, placidly following, with a rare trot to catch up to the others and give me a chance to ride 'western' without posting."

Eleanor arrived as scheduled and was so thrilled with Jasper that I forbore to compare it with Maligne. We went on together out to Prince Rupert, and down to Vancouver by boat. There we parted briefly. She had a heart interest to test, and I wanted to visit Florrie Hicks at her apple ranch in the Okanagan. When we met again it was to begin our three weeks' camping on the summit of Mount Revelstoke. Curry had pioneered this with one of her students the year before. The parents of this student lent us what we needed and drove us up through dense fog to the square, glass-sided lookout cabin that was to be our headquarters.

"Up and up in the truck, through clouds, seeing glimpses of the town, of other mountains, through huge timber with hanging branches, past four-mile cabin, eight-mile cabin, all the cabins, up and up till there was just scrub growth, and little Balsam Lake, and then the lookout ahead, perched like a red-and-white doll's house on the very top." The clouds that were covering our mountain gradually thinned and began to dissipate, opening up views of other ranges and the valley of the Columbia River, fresh marvels with each gap in the clouds. We pitched a tent on the meadow below to satisfy the technicalities, but we ate, slept, and worked in the main room of the lookout. On weekends, town visitors and tourists moved freely across us and up into the tower. The rest of the time we were left in peace, with a daily call from the warden of the park to bring us mail and supplies and drink the good coffee we brewed. Our duty was to watch for fires and report them.

One night, just at dusk, we saw one start on the edge of one of the mountains, and even as we watched we could see the orange flame spread and glow. The nearest telephone was at eight-mile cabin, a long way down. We ran. It was all downhill, and in not more than five or six minutes we were there and able to get the warden on the telephone. It took us much longer to climb back up, with big grins on our red faces. The warden had assured us that our "forest fire" was the rising full moon.

My diary is full of complaints about the bad sketches I was making, but it later reports a quite successful exhibition of them and the canvases based on them. I am still learning that my paintings are always disasters while I am doing them. It isn't until I see them later, and someone else likes them, that I can see their virtues.

Tragic news from home cut short our summer. Ken's wife, Betty, died very suddenly of heart exhaustion during one of her recurrent attacks of asthma. Ken's letter made me decide to reroute my return trip through Toledo. He wanted to see me.

That was the year of the terrible epidemic of poliomyelitis in Ontario. The Toronto schools remained closed until mid-September, and, after I had come back from my visit with Ken, Curry and I had a rare opportunity to paint the autumn colours. We lived in one of her brother Ron's summer cottages on Hall's Lake in Haliburton, and painted and painted.

We paid for those weeks of freedom by a lengthened school day, "with school getting worse and worse every minute with an increase of time, and tightening of details and a growing sense of pressure. I am fed up. Except that along with it this year has come the new course of study that lets us try expressive illustration and for me marionettes! I'm having fun with them."

16

Heartstrings

IT WAS THE MEMORY of the Punch and Judy show at Hampstead Heath that made me keen to try out puppetry with a group of art students. These were comparatively mature students, high school graduates. The first day I met them, I suggested that they toss around some ideas for plots that they might use, bearing in mind that each of them would make, dress, and operate one character and share the responsibility for scenery and furnishings. The students were to come next week with penknives for carving the heads out of balsa-wood, a very light wood from South America that can be cut easily. By the end of the afternoon there were three plays planned and parts decided: a hillbilly melodrama featuring an evil landlord with designs on the virtue of the daughter of the house, Jack and the Beanstalk, and an episode of the Tarzan story.

Making the marionettes involved thinking three-

dimensionally and functionally, not only establishing the
proportions of the body, human or animal, but also an-
alysing the movements necessary for head, torso, legs,
and arms, and designing appropriate joints. Feet had to
move up and down at the ankle but turn only slightly from
side to side. Legs must be able to swing forward up to the
head, but less freely backward. Knees should not twist
sideways. Arms are more complex because the wrist
moves at right angles to the action of the elbow, while the
shoulder is capable of swinging in a complete circle. Arm,
legs, and hands were carved from pine, with metal pins
through the joints, or with leather hinges, loose or tight
depending on how much flexibility was needed. I think
this was when I really learned the lessons of drawing that
the teachers in London had tried so hard to teach me. I
began to think structurally and functionally, and to teach
the students to think this way. I began to appreciate the
human body as a series of simple cylindrical parts, of
differing proportions, some tapering more than others,
dependent on a basically solid rectangular shoulder and
a basically solid rectangular hip, these two rectangles
capable of bending and twisting in relation to each other.
We learned to think of the head as a sphere that lengthened in front to a face with the two sides set at a characteristic angle, the features less important than the basic
structure.

The naked puppets were already full of personality.
Their balsa-wood heads lolled against their wooden
shoulders. Their cloth midriffs collapsed, leaving shoulders and hips at odd angles. Their hands were carved with
clumsy fists or with delicate fingers suggesting the character to come. Feet from the beginning were made with

high-heeled slippers or heavy boots, whatever was demanded by the role. By the time they were dressed, they
were already "in the part." Before we were through that
first season of puppetry I had taught (and sometimes had
to learn) how to weave a straw hat, the anatomy of a
gorilla, pattern drafting for men's and women's clothing,
wig-making, stage design, research into periods of furniture and dress styles, voice production, diction, stage
movement and its relation to character and mood, tailor-
ing, and dressmaking.

We were committed to producing the three plays as a
feature of the annual spring bazaar, a sort of open house
when the school brought the public in to see what a
technical school was all about and made a few dollars by
selling baked goods, pottery, and tickets for the auditorium show. That show had acquired an enviable reputation for professional finish. We were challenged to
maintain that standard with ours.

Added to all the usual director's nightmares was the
mechanical perversity of the actors: joints that came
apart, leaving a leg hanging by itself in mid-air, screw-
eyes that fell out of the soft balsa-wood, strings that
tangled. Balancing such disasters was the unexpected
strength of the personalities of the little creatures. They
became people, and we fell in love with them.

The other great difficulty was the attraction they had
for every student who could drift out of the class he
should have been in and sneak in to watch the rehearsals.
My classroom was a madhouse. Normal timetables went
by the board in the pressure of last-minute preparations
for the big day, and my room became the catch-all for the
human flotsam of the department.

Through all the confusion the core workers repaired marionettes, revised the design of joints, untangled the nine five-foot lengths of nylon fish-line, rehearsed lines between sessions on the stage, and practised manipulating the control bars to achieve realistic movements of the head and hands, so that the puppet looked as if he were talking when his lines were being said by the invisible operator, and the other puppets on stage looked as if they were listening.

That first year we were rewarded by ready laughter and the surprise of people who came backstage afterwards. They saw the marionettes hanging from the controls and exclaimed, "But surely the ones on the stage were much bigger!"

There were other years when we did *Romeo and Juliet* and *Uncle Tom's Cabin*, expecting them to be hilariously funny. They turned out to be poetic instead, and touching. The operators of the marionettes in *Uncle Tom's Cabin* had good voices and musical taste. Their use of Negro spirituals between scenes and sometimes as part of a scene was very moving. From the darkness of the bridge above the stage we heard the peculiar quality of the hush that fell on the audience, and the nose-blowing afterwards. As relief from this, beautiful Liza with her infant in her arms, leaping from ice floe to ice floe in the midst of a wildly agitated green cloth river, and pursued by two baying cloth hounds, all flopping ears and heaving rear ends, was comic as well as exciting.

Our tour de force, however, was the show that used teachers as the characters, and Heaven as the setting. Peter Haworth, in deference to his status as head of the department, became Saint Peter, dressed like all the

others in a long white nightie with realistically painted
wings, his characteristic head with its curly fair hair quite
unmistakable. He was centre stage at a table and chair,
in charge of the Pearly Gates, which stood behind him
against a blue sky with floating clouds. Mrs. Jutton –
dear sweet vague Mrs. Jutton, who was always looking
for her keys – poked her head out over the gate, to report
the keys of Heaven missing. Familiar figures flew in,
seeking admission from Saint Peter. Carl Schaefer, his
unruly shock of hair over his eyes as usual, his boom-
boom voice taking himself very seriously as usual, protested the delay, but to no avail. Mully soared in, too
interested in his algebraic calculations of the distance
from earth to worry about the lost keys. Crichty floated
down, her grey hair immaculately coiffed, her Scottish
accent well mimicked. Charlie Goldhamer arrived, an
excellent likeness with a clever piece of Persian lamb to
exaggerate the tidiness of his short curly hair. Bob Ross
was a notorious non-conformist among the staff, known
to smell of alcohol sometimes, even in school hours, but
a terrific teacher of life drawing and very popular with
his students. He came, hiding the keys behind his back,
using them as a bribe to get the doors to open even for
him. Bob was behind the scenes, playing himself. When
the Pearly Gates finally opened wide it was to reveal the
back of the school organist, George Graham, with his
familiar patent-leather hair, seated on a bench at the
console of a huge pipe organ, as we saw him in the
auditorium every week. He provided the triumphant
music that brought the scene to a close. This skit was well
received at the official performances, but it was on the
Monday afterwards, when we repeated the show for the

students who had been on duty and unable to see it before, that it came into its own. Then, every nuance of voice, every remembered gesture or mannerism was received with a roar of laughter.

The summer after Betty's death, Mother had Ken's three motherless children up at the cabin, and I joined them there for weekends. Doug and Audrey bridged the chasm that had opened up between Mother and themselves and brought young Dale to join his cousins at the cottage. Grandfather was there. Grace had left us and not been replaced. Marjorie's mother, newly widowed, took a cottage nearby, with Marjorie and baby Anne. That was the summer that Marjorie and I were able to revisit Silver Island.

We took off together and paddled the eight miles or so back to the familiar landmarks, past Mortimer's Point, past Eddie Mortimer's farm and the Kettles, where the water was still boiling over the rocks, on to Dunbarton and at last to Silver Island. We paused at Ferriers' cottage for the courtesies, as we had on our first arrival, then went up the familiar path to Spyglass. There we scrabbled in the mulch of pine needles and earth at the base of the trunk until we found it. It was still there, the screw-top jar with the note we had written in that golden past. We laughed at it, of course, at its pre-teen solemnity. We knew that we had already carried the treasure away from the island and would have it with us for the rest of our lives.

Nory and I were teaching puppetry to the teachers' summer course at Central Tech. Between weekends I

lived a casual life at home, roller-skating with my CTS
puppeteers, dancing at the parties they threw, and giving
a couple of notable parties myself, when I mixed the art
students with my Shawnees and some of the student
teachers and found that they combined well.

It was at one of those gatherings that Betty's mother
made a memorable remark. Betty Priestly was one of my
CGIT group, and also a student in the art department. Her
mother and I were checking up on the dining-room table,
to see that it was ready for the festivities, when I noticed
the cobweb hanging from the ceiling and exclaimed in
dismay.

"They can form overnight," she consoled me. "But,"
she added, looking again, "they don't turn black overnight." I made sure that the cobwebs were gone before
Mother came home.

That fall, Dawson Kennedy and I chaperoned a house
party of art students for a weekend of sketching at Barbara Browne's cottage on Lake Erie. "October 29, 1938:
The weekend at Turkey Point was memorable for two
things, first and most of all, a return to Normandale. I was
suddenly swamped with memories. It seemed tiny, but
unbelievably well-known. Every little irregularity in the
ground was familiar. I felt all my sixteen- and seventeen-
year-old emotion flooding back. It was all immediate and
real instead of a half-sentimental memory. I found myself
not in the least amused by my teen-age self, rather more
appalled by my grown-up one. How earnest and how
determined we were, and how gay, and it seems particularly bitter as I remember that this September we were
closer to war than I have ever known. For weeks we lived
with the cold certainty of disaster coming, watching the

world move towards annihilation – and even yet I feel the
fear clutching me. Just lately the papers have had an
ominous sound that makes me wonder if it were only a
delay."

The other event was a frank talk with Walter Fraser,
who came for the weekend. His young wife had died after
childbirth, and he was once more courting. But I had
grown far beyond the girl he had known in Hamilton.
Walter was disappointed and hurt, but had to accept my
firm "Sorry, but no." Our ways parted again.

It was that fall, at the end of a Saturday sketching with
Betty Priestly and Madeline Glenn, another Shawnee, a
few miles east of Toronto at Rosebank, that I saw a vacant
cottage that reminded me how much I wanted a place to
call my own. There was a For Sale sign on it. We walked
around it, peering in the windows that we could reach,
and on the way home called in to see the real estate agent
whose name was on the sign. I told him what interested
me about it and what I really didn't like. He said that he
knew of another that might suit me better, and made a
date to show it to me. This was a small stucco cottage, on
a steep wooded slope above a long grassy meadow. The
meadow lay between two ravines on a stretch of Scarborough Bluffs cut off by the ravines from any road access.
From the cottage I could see a small woods beside the
ravine on the left. "What about that land down there?" I
asked. "Is it for sale?" I didn't like the idea that someone
below me could someday cut me off from the lake. Mr.
White admitted that it was also for sale.

"November 2: I'm too excited tonight to bear it alone.
Today we went crashing around in the weeds and thorns
and burrs and ended up in a heavenly spot, twelve acres

on the corner between the bluffs and a great lovely ravine, nature on three sides, my beautiful lake, the ravine, the broad fields like Normandale. It's a perfect spot! And it's mine for $1,500. I have abandoned a new car and a year abroad with scarcely a backward glance, except to assure the year abroad that it's just postponed. Height! Woods! Lake! Please, birds. And as someone reminded me tonight, probably poison ivy."

I drew house plans and dreamed dreams. Mother labelled it "that fool's paradise of yours," and I put it in capital letters and made it official. I dragged all my friends out to see it and pass judgement, and then the blow fell. The realtor raised the price, and my dreams crashed to the ground. For the rest of the winter and the spring I stayed away, viewing it only from the hill across the ravine, feeling that my eagerness had betrayed me. Before school ended in the spring of 1939 I asked a lawyer friend to get in touch with the realtor again and demand his final price, with no more nonsense. This time it was reduced to $1,250, a road down the hill and along the flat to reach it was thrown in, and Ted closed the deal while I was up north.

Paradise lost and paradise regained, and, best of all, Marjorie and Roy were moving back to Toronto. Roy had been accepted for a teaching post at our old school, Malvern.

In August I returned to serious painting up at Georgian Bay. It was on the drive home from there, after pausing for Labour Day weekend at the Muskoka cabin where there was no radio, that we stopped at a little roadside stand to buy cigarettes and heard that war had been declared. Nory wept all the rest of the way home. I drove, with face set, trying not to realize what it might mean. For many months it meant very little beyond a constant anxiety and the routine as usual. The Major was in the army almost at once, but that was all we knew about him.

I was spending weekends at Fool's Paradise, tenting on the edge of the bluffs and cooking on an open fire. Del and Jimmy Thorne shared it with me most times. Del was the young woman who had been recommended to me as a helper when I agreed to reorganize the Sunday school at St. Aidan's. She and Jimmy had become my close friends, welcomed by Mother for the bridge games they made possible, ready for any adventure I suggested. Their little apartment on Queen Street was a dependable refuge when I needed to get away from home.

Then, in the spring of 1940, the German blitzkrieg swept across Europe, and France fell, and the war became as terrifying as our nightmares.

"Thursday, May 30, 1940: It's still Paradise, although all this week I've been afraid even to think about it. Tuesday was a dreadful day. So far from cutting the German advance in two, the British were being trapped by it, and still are, but by now the shock of it has exhausted my powers of worry, and I'm numb again. Tuesday none of us could do any work. We stood about in the halls and argued, savagely, that it couldn't be – and that there seemed no hope of it not being. I couldn't phone White about the road. It seemed too incredibly trivial, and I was wondering whether I ought not to be buying war bonds instead of building. But tonight Del and I drove out after supper. It was a grey evening, the woods seemed to be all in blossom because of the silvery grey of the young poplar leaves. The well goes in a clean dry shaft forever down, and not a sign of water yet. Curse the silly willow wand! Then we leaned over the ravine edge looking down to where the willows are showing young leaves more than an inch long. As we lay there, marvelling at the beautiful rich foliage down in the ravine, a thrush sang, and my cup of happiness seemed full."

Nory and George were married that summer, too late to save him from being drafted into the army. Betty Priestly and I were bridesmaids in pink chiffon, twice, because Nory and George had adopted the Baha'i religion and went through a Baha'i service a couple of days after the conventional one in a church. George was soon in uniform. Nory, being married, was dismissed from her job at Tech as expected, but once night school opened in September, Peter was able to hire her for a couple of classes a week.

It was that summer that Ken remarried. After Betty's untimely death, he had depended on housekeepers to care for the children, with occasional help from Aunt Shirley, Betty's younger sister. Shirley Caswell was a graduate nurse who had frequently stayed with them in Toledo to see Betty through her bouts of asthma. We were all delighted with their decision to marry.

I had some interesting dates that year, usually cookouts over the little brick fireplace in the woods at Fool's Paradise, but none of them developed into more than friendship. Marjorie had her second baby, John, and was increasingly cocooned in diapers, bottles, and toys. Walter found himself a new wife and again became Mother's white-haired boy. Of me, Mother remarked to my friends, gathered for a dinner before one of the art gallery

openings, "Oh, nobody would marry *her*." And so it
seemed.

But the remark troubled Del and angered her. She
scolded me for letting Mother bully me the way she did.
I recognized the justice of her protest, but I also understood Mother's fear of losing me, and realized that the
remark was intended as a reminder to me that I was
damaged goods, a Bad Girl. Two nights later a young
medical intern, a photographer, who was working with
me to produce a poster for CGIT's big anniversary cele-
bration, came down to the house for a conference after
work. Since he was on duty at the hospital until ten, it
was almost eleven when he arrived. I had tea ready for
him in the studio, and we worked out the details of the
poster satisfactorily. At twelve-thirty, as he was leaving,
Mother appeared at the head of the stairs in her dressing-
gown, in a fury. "Do you know what time it is?" After I
had hustled Lloyd out she had more to say, concluding
with "Never ask that man here again."

I didn't argue. But I didn't sleep. I could find no
excuses for her. Lloyd was a gentleman, eminently eligible. I was thirty years old. In the morning I went into
Mother's room and put my case. It was her house. She
had a right to make the rules, but I was going to have to
move out if she would not agree to let me choose my
friends and bring them to the house without having them
embarrassed or treated with rudeness. "Think it over."

When I came home that night I asked for her decision.
"I don't know what you are talking about," said Mother.
"I meant what I said," I replied. "Don't be ridiculous" was
her last word.

A week later I had found a space, still at the Beach, in a bungalow with a widow who was glad of someone in the house and able to clear her rooms so that I could bring my own furniture. The big rec room in the cellar was studio and living room. Her laundry, beside it, was my kitchen, and we shared the bathroom between our bedrooms on the main floor. A side entrance leading up or down gave me real privacy. For seven years we were comfortable house-mates, independent but supportive.

I called often at home, hoping that Mother would modify her implacable silence. Grandfather was always glad to see me. He regretted my moving out and missed me but never reproached me. Mary, who had followed Grace (but not replaced her), was an unimaginative woman who offered him no genial companionship. She is memorable to me chiefly for her remark over some news item in the paper: "God might forgive murder, but I'm sure He would never forgive adultery." Of all the friends and relations, the only one to protest was Doug, and, considering that he had found three months under Mother's roof intolerable, I was not impressed.

Charlie Goldhamer and Carl Schaefer left the art department to become war artists. Virginia Luz, slim, dark, pleasant, and a former student, was taken on to handle Nory's timetable of classes in illustration. I had more senior drawing and painting classes than before, and two rooms to look after – challenging, but rewarding too. Dawson was a tower of strength, more and more appreciated as the pressure mounted. He developed a course in camouflage to make his design and colour theory more obviously relevant. We were the two directed to take the hastily organized summer courses in "defence" so that we could teach home nursing, first aid, camp-craft, internal combustion engines, nutrition, and aircraft recognition, all considered important in case of invasion. I hadn't realized that there were still so many fields of knowledge not covered by puppetry.

There was a proposal to take over the school for a training centre for soldiers, and for several weeks we taught surrounded by the cardboard cartons in which we had hastily packed the contents of all our cupboards and storerooms. Mercifully, that plan was shelved in favour of keeping the school open twenty-four hours a day and running training courses for the armed forces in two shifts during the night.

It must have been a year later that Virginia Luz and I were walking along the corridor on C floor, on our way to the teachers' dining room, reminding each other to say that we were "beautiful and beloved," which someone had told us was the infallible recipe for walking well. There was a big white balloon lying on the floor, which we rescued and carried into the dining room with us. The art department and Jimmie Dean and Mully filled the first table inside the door. We bopped Peter on the head with the balloon, someone seized it and threw it in the air, and it went from hand to hand around the room and disappeared among the shopmen. After lunch, Ginny and I went together to Peter's office for some reason, in time to hear him answer the telephone and start to laugh. We watched him turn bright red. He pulled his face to an exaggerated solemnity and promised that it would never happen again.

"That was the principal," he said to us severely. "He was shocked by the behaviour of the two young ladies in the art department." But he couldn't keep his face straight any longer, as he told us that the principal had identified our noon-hour balloon as an inflated "safe."

Those war years, with the few of us carrying extra loads, were gruelling. But the worst year followed the summer that Peter and his wife had spent out west, flying from airfield to airfield, painting the installations and the life of the RCAF. During the First World War Peter had been shot down, wounded, and badly shell-shocked. I doubt if either he or Bobs had anticipated how hard it would be on his nerves to go back to so much flying. He returned from that summer exhausted, edgy, unreason-able, and more demanding than ever. His teachers had learned long since never to argue or defend themselves with him. It was best to take it in silence and wait for tomorrow, when he would be over his anger and might even be able to laugh with you at his display of temper. But that year strained our endurance.

There was one winter afternoon when I said with more than usual fervour, "Thank God it's Friday." After a long tough week, Peter came into one of my classrooms, an-noyed about some work or equipment that I had stored in the cupboard at the back of the room. He gave me a thorough dressing-down in front of my class, which the students ignored, going on with their work in embar-rassed silence. I apologized and promised to reorganize the cupboard completely as soon as possible. The stu-dents were as aware as I of the enormity of Peter's attack, but we all carried on without comment. When I was back in my other classroom for roll call at the end of the afternoon, he turned up again, this time to complain that some drawing-boards had been left on the tables. I assured him that they would be put away properly, and began tidying them up. When I had inspected both rooms again and was sure that even Peter couldn't find a further nit to pick, I dressed, ready to leave, and called in at his office to collect Ginny and say good night. Peter looked at me and said, "Where in God's name did you get that hat?" at which point I burst into tears. Ginny followed me into Peter's washroom to help me regain control and dry myself up. When she left me and returned to Peter, he asked innocently, "What's the matter with her?" Ginny said it was a terrible hat, but no more terrible than Peter's wartime technique with his staff.

One summer afternoon two years after I had moved away from home, Roy Wood drove out to Fool's Paradise to tell me that Grandpa had been stricken with a heart attack and that Mother was up at Mrs. McGill's cottage at Lake Simcoe. The doctor had been called. The dear old man was already heavily sedated when I got to the house, but he knew me. I sat holding his hand until early evening when Mother reached home and ordered me out of the house. I protested, unable to believe that she could be so cruel, but there was no relenting. He died that night. Mother even refused to tell me the funeral arrangements, which I knew would not be at St. Aidan's. But she could not prevent my finding out that she had booked the crematorium, and I went by myself to sit through the service, alone at the back of the chapel.

17

Two Loves

WHEN LOVE CAME it caught me unawares. For many years we had been associated in one way or another in the educational world, and increasingly friends. We worked well together and enjoyed each other, but then, everyone loved him. He was a comfortable, understanding person, intelligent, with a notable sense of humour, and enough foibles that one laughed at him as well as with him. I could talk to him about things that were important to me, and he listened. I had often met his wife socially, assumed a good marriage, and had no thought of complications ahead.

One late afternoon we had been working on a job that was taxing, concentrated, and creative. When the meeting wound up and the others took off, we were ready to find a retreat under the trees, to talk it over and share a sociable cigarette before we also went our ways. It was October at its most genial, golden in the warm sun. His

kiss was gentle, but its effect was metamorphic. I drove
down to Fool's Paradise in a turmoil of surprise and
recognition, tenderness and terror.

Living in my own little flat had given me back the
freedom of my diary, and I wrote out the emotions of
those first tormented up-and-down months. I fought
against falling into such a profitless love, struggling to be
content with companionship, lying awake nights in anger
and despair, weeping on Marjorie's shoulder and leaning
on Del's sympathy. An hour alone with him raised me to
heaven and blew my firm resolutions to the winds.

"November 6: In bed, with an ache in me that seems
to start at the heart and permeate in all directions. I know
it's right to decide never to see him alone, and I'm glad it's
done, and I'm more terrified of going on than of stopping,
but I still feel the way I did the week war was declared,
as if my world had suddenly fallen apart, and I'm sick
with loneliness and fear, fear of my own weakness even
as then. I think Del and M in their conversation over the
telephone today planned a mud campaign, and I'm glad
they didn't need it." I had been able to tell them that we
had already agreed to stop seeing each other.

It was proof of his goodness that he had not pressured
me. "All I did was make one small plea. I hardly even
needed to make it. My own misery was all my argument,
and I met understanding and kindness and tenderness
and co-operation. I wondered this afternoon if any of my
Pre-vocational boys noticed their teacher leaning against
the window with her eyes full of tears."

Of course it wasn't as easy as that. The renunciation
didn't last. I was pulled this way and that all fall. We both
struggled and tried to help each other. Our love grew in

secret, and we came to accept secrecy as the price we had to pay. It was finally a considered decision, made after counselling by a wise woman who was also a doctor, that we would welcome this rare gift that life was offering us, and become lovers in deed. I am forever grateful for that decision. We knew passionate mutuality, unfailing understanding, a heightening of every shared occasion, and as there were still constant opportunities to work together, constant situations that could involve us both, we saw each other often. I had not been an actress all my life for nothing, and his normally impassive face could be an effective mask. Everyone loved him, so our friendly companionship was unremarkable. We were discreet.

So it went for half a year, until a crisis in his family wrenched us apart. "Do you want me to pretend it never happened?" I asked, "because I can." Nightmare weeks followed. I was completely hollow, a shell going through the motions of living. I can still relive the winter Saturday when at last he telephoned and I flew to meet him, to be held in his arms to sob out my desolation on his shoulder.

But I couldn't live on one hour in six months. In desperation I wondered if it was love I needed instead of him, and for the first (and last) time in my life I picked out an eligible man and made a play for him. He was a sweet fellow, a young doctor whose first-aid course I attended at the Beaches Library. He rose like a fish to bait, which I found somewhat comforting in my emptiness. He was on the rebound after having been refused by a girl he had courted for some years, and he was as willing to fall in love as I was. He even took me home to his father's farm to meet the family, and the approval was mutual. But although our affair ambled along for more than six months, neither of us found what we were looking for and we parted by mutual consent. This was not even a ghost of what I had known with my darling.

I have forgotten the slow steps by which he and I crept together again. We were even more cautious, more discreet, but neither one of us could sustain the separation. For six years after that, we were together, often, hungrily, our friendship as important to us as our love. I am a good actress but a poor liar, and it was very hard for me to be less than candid with the friends who were close to me. Marjorie and Del knew about us and had become sympathetic and co-operative. But there was the Saturday morning that two other friends arrived at Fool's Paradise on their bicycles when I was expecting my beloved, and I told them that I wanted to be alone and sent them away. That still shames me.

The time came when I was no longer able to content myself with the half-loaf. I wanted marriage, his children, to walk arm in arm with him with my head high. Soon it would be time to move into my Scarborough home and start a permanent life there. I was tired of half-truths and evasions. The circumstances of his life at that time made me feel that he could break with his wife without involving me. It seemed to me to be now or never.

When it became apparent that it was not to be now, that he could not take the difficult step, I decided that we must go back to being just friends. I practised saying, "I don't need him, to hell with him," while I weeded the garden. It wasn't very convincing, but it was an attempt to practise what I have come to believe, that if you act the way you wish you felt, you will eventually come to feel that way.

I made the rules, that we should be in private as we were in public, with no more lovemaking, no more intimate talk. This time we both respected the conditions, which left us free to feel however we chose but bound us to behave by the book. And in all the years of friendship that we enjoyed after that, a friendship that came to include his wife, we continued to know the marvellous comfort of each other's understanding and affection.

I have no regrets. It had taken some rationalizing to reconcile what we were doing with the stern sexual standards of the church. But I believe now, as I believed then, that the kind of love that cares for the other person more than for oneself is not sin in the eyes of God. I also know that it takes real toughness to defy a social taboo, and this was the toughness that I had but that he could not summon.

The other love of my life was born at the same time and has continued to grow. It was the very day of that first kiss that I drove down the track (it could hardly be called a road) to Fool's Paradise and found the skeletal outline of a house, floor joists in place and the framework of the outside walls. Before the snow fell it was roofed and sheathed, with windows in place and a door that locked, a little white box of a house with a blue roof, set up on brick posts and looking as if the first strong wind would blow it away. The well had been dug down fifty-two feet before finding water, and beside it was the mountain of clay, sand, and stones that had come out of it. Working by the bucketful, I used that pile of earth to build flowerbeds around the house to hide the foundation posts, and eventually to give the driveway a crown that would keep it dry. The well-rounded boulders that came out of the well, souvenirs of Lake Iroquois in prehistoric times, made my first rock garden around the blue hand-pump that delivered water from the well from time to time and refused to deliver it almost as often. There was no money for plants, but so many friends brought baskets of perennial roots and envelopes of seeds that I could hardly keep up with the planting. The government offered trees for reforestation. My friends and my students came to plant the steep slopes of the bluffs and the ravine with willow twigs to fight the erosion.

Forest Telfer was my builder. It was his mother-in-law who had taken me into her bungalow when I left home, and he was already a friend. He had such sympathy for my vision of a dream home that he gave me the stone-faced fireplace that I had decided I could not afford. Although the house was little more than a shell, its appearance satisfied the zoning regulations. The area was restricted to single-family dwellings of a value of at least twenty-five hundred dollars, considered a respectable sum in those days. Without electricity and running water I couldn't hope to use it except as a cottage, but during the war years I worked away at the inside, managing to insulate it, have it wired, line it with knotty pine, and build shelves and cupboards, so that if and when life returned to normal, I could make it my permanent home.

Water had been found in a stratum of very fine sand, and this sand seeped through the brick lining of the well and was drawn up into the pump, clogging it. My well had been dug by a local well-digger and one assistant. They worked with shovels, digging a clean, accurate, round shaft about three feet in diameter that went down and down, then lining it with bricks laid without mortar. The pump stood on a platform down in the depths, because it was far too deep a well for a pump to pull the water. It had to push it up. By the second summer Bill Smith, my well-digger, was in a war production factory, his assistant gone, and I was desperate for dependable water. Bill was sympathetic, but there was no way he could pour a cement lining for the bottom six feet of that well without help. It was a triumph that he agreed to use me as his assistant.

Bill was an unregenerate old Scot from Glasgow, without formal education, colourful of speech, full of stories about the days when he was "on pogey." He was a careful workman, establishing the winch firmly above the opening, using good new rope, too careful and too experienced to trust me to handle the winch. Instead, I was lowered on a sling into the well, down onto the platform, and with a saucepan upside down on my head as a hard hat, I received the buckets of cement that Bill mixed and let down to me. I shovelled them into the wooden form he had built inside the brick lining. A touch of comedy was Bill's "Miss McCarthy" when I was up on top, which changed to "Doris" when I was down the hole and he was hollering instructions or asking if I wanted to come up for a cigarette.

From that time on, Bill was my friend, keeping an eye on the cottage and available for labouring jobs as need arose. For several more years I moved from one emergency to another. There was current at the time a hilarious film called *Mr. Blandings Builds His Dream House*, highly recommended. I avoided it. I had lived through too many bitter experiences of shock and disappointment to laugh at somebody else's troubles.

I can't imagine when I had time for painting, but I did big water-colours of the marionettes in action, water-colours of the garden flowers that were bursting into bloom around me, and snow canvases of Haliburton, which was still my refuge at Christmas and Easter. I even spent part of the summer of 1941 down on the Gaspé coast being an artist instead of a householder. Early in the war I had one-man shows at the Beaches Library, at Wymilwood (a women's residence at Victoria College), and at Mellor's Gallery before it became the Roberts Gallery. I always showed in the juried exhibitions of the societies.

Way back in the Thirties I had achieved the necessary three consecutive acceptances in the annual juried show of the Ontario Society of Artists and had approached Fred Haines, then the president, to suggest that I was now eligible for membership. He seemed amused at the temerity of this young girl in aspiring to such a height and sent me away abashed. But in wartime, with many of the men off serving as war artists, women began to have a higher profile. My 1944 solo show at Wymilwood was followed by one at Simpson's, which was given some publicity and well attended. It was then that Alan Collier asked me why I was not a member of the OSA, and he sounded comfortingly indignant when I told him. The next spring I was duly elected to membership, proudly able to sign OSA after my name and to attend the monthly meetings at the Arts and Letters Club with all the greats. A.J. Casson had succeeded Fred Brigden, L.A.C. Panton, and Frank Carmichael as president, with George Pepper, Jack Bush, and Sid Hallam as vice-presidents in the offing, and York Wilson, Cleeve Horne, Sydney Watson, and Peter Haworth ready to take over the presidency when the time came. They were a strong group. Membership was a tremendous stimulus to me as a painter. Recognition by my peers meant far more to me than sales, which were still hardly enough to cover the cost of frames.

My first venture into modernism was an abstraction of Fool's Paradise and the bluffs, with the angel that had become my logo. One afternoon up at the Delicious, the Greek restaurant where students and teachers used to gather for a cuppa after school, Bob Ross had done a scribble of an angel on a paper serviette for me. I carved it in pine to be my weathervane, and it continues to appear on rugs, in mobiles, and in paintings. It dominated this recklessly (for me) modern canvas, which was accepted for the OSA juried exhibition and earned a press mention. Great excitement!

Carving puppet parts had introduced me to the pleasure of a sharp knife and a block of clean-grained pine. To keep my hands busy while my puppeteers worked, I had carved myself the figures for a Christmas crèche. Dawson Kennedy was knowledgeable in such things and taught me the medieval method of polychrome finish over a gesso base, as well as the careful craftsmanship needed to paint miniature gems set in gold filigree on kings' crowns. For Christmas, I made another set for Marjorie, and later, others for Del and Nancy Caudle. Nancy was my fellow artist, a friend since high school, who was now living at the Beach and had become part of my life at St. Aidan's.

It was normal for me to carry the figure-in-progress wherever I went, with the knife and a kerchief to catch the chips. I carved while I visited. Basil English, "the Doc" to his friends, was the young rector who had succeeded Dr. Cotton at St. Aidan's. He asked me to carve a large set for the church. I agreed, on condition that the church provide the wood. This was to be laminated pine, two-inch slabs bonded with the grain at right angles. I was poor. Mother had withdrawn her promised loan to finance Fool's Paradise, and I was in debt to the bank and squeezing pennies.

For three years I worked away at those figures, graduating to chisels and U-shaped gouges, but too diffident to use power tools. I had to feel my way slowly, and hand-carving suited my pace. It took me a year to finish the Holy Family. I had designed Mary as a young peasant girl, kneeling at the side of the manger, one hand ready to draw her veil across her face. Joseph's hands are together in the gesture of prayer. And by a chance that pleases me still, Joseph looks like my father. It is a better likeness than any photograph I have of Dad. In imitation of Renaissance paintings, the Babe was made wide-eyed. Nancy and Del protested that this was not right for a newborn. So now we have two Babes, the second one truly an infant, the original one replacing it at Epiphany. The next year I added three shepherds, using my cat as a model to help me with the anatomy of the lamb in the arms of one of them, and a year later the three Magi were complete. Evenings when I would be working away at the block of wood, which rocked on the cushion under it with each drive of the chisel, the chips flying and piling deeper on the floor, Lady Macbeth's words would keep echoing in my mind, "Who would have thought the old man to have had so much blood in him?"

Eventually, I decided to add two kneeling angels, as supporters. One of them was soon ready to paint, the other is still waiting to be completed thirty-five years later. I remind my friends that many people consider Michelangelo's unfinished "prisoners" to be his master-pieces.

The war worsened. One of the curates at St. Aidan's, who had a rural background, surprised me by getting a friend of his to plough up a large piece of the field at Fool's Paradise. I had no choice but to plant it. This plunged me into one of the happy periods, with the Bennetts (Madeline Glenn Bennett, one of my Shawnees, and her husband), the Lobbs (friends of theirs and now of mine), the Kennedys (Kath and Dawson), and eventually Doug and Audrey, all with substantial victory gardens outside my door. Saturdays there were at least half a dozen of us hoeing away and gathering for lunch in the screened porch. One fruitful October the Kennedys gave a harvest party for all of us, and I was presented with a fine big cross-cut saw.

Every autumn after that, on one of the days when the school was given a half-holiday to attend a rugby game, I would call for the Doc at the Beach and take him out to Fool's Paradise for an afternoon of labour. There were some huge oaks in the woods up back of the field. One had fallen in a storm, and we worked away in a steady rhythm, back and forth, back and forth, cutting it into segments that could be drawn on a toboggan back to the house and eventually split. Sometimes Kay, Basil's gorgeous wife, was with us, and she would have supper under way by the time we had finished with the cutting. Otherwise, Basil lit the fire in the living room while I made one in the kitchen range, and after supper we sat with our feet towards the hearth and a drink in our hands, and he read aloud the wisdom he had chosen for the day. I remember best *The Screwtape Letters* by C.S. Lewis, for its wit, and because each of us was able to recognize himself or the other in Lewis's shrewd descriptions of the devices of the Devil to tempt us to folly or worse.

As soon as I was able to get furniture into the house I planned the annual Christmas party that became an institution. The famous one took place on the Saturday night in 1942 that the temperature plunged to thirty-five below zero Fahrenheit. The morning was already very cold. I telephoned around from my Neville Park flat to assess the prospects, and we decided to carry on. Virginia Luz, a friend by this time, had stayed with me overnight, so we collected Del and Ruth Peters, loaded the food and the decorations into the car along with the toboggan, and drove out to the top of the hill. It was half a mile down the hill and along to the cottage, through heavy snow, with a wind that whipped the top off the box of paper angels and sent them flying through the air. In spite of sunshine, the inside of the cottage was below zero when we arrived.

The first job was a fire, and we piled on the wood to make a blaze that would fill the hearth and heat the room. Ginny, standing with her back to it to feel its warmth, smelled the back of her new fur coat as it singed across the seat. By dusk, when the rest of the party came, the living room was almost comfortable, the tree decked with angels, the food ready, table set, candles everywhere, a sight to warm the hearts and even the bodies. The gallon of wine on the porch had frozen. We poured off the alcohol and sipped it. Distillation by frost. I washed dishes in a pan on the almost red-hot stove in the kitchen, but the water that ran off the hot dishes onto the kitchen table froze as it reached it. Del did her famous ballet number, which was orthodox enough to be wildly funny. We sang carols. Joe Peters told his story of the Christmas tree that was rebuilt branch by branch and twig by swig (with predictable results). But we could not quite forget the cars parked up at the top of the hill in the bitter cold. We packed up early and began the trudge up through the snow.

One of the engines started. Into that car we handed Peggy Laskin and Ruth, our two pregnant women, and Marjorie Johnson, who had a lame back. George drove them off in that car. We were not to know that they got only as far as the first garage before the radiator boiled over and they were stranded. We pushed a second car down the road to the highway. A helpful bus driver gave it a push and it started. Nory and Nancy Caudle were with Bora Laskin and Joe Peters in that one. The rest of us tried in vain to get my car to move. After all day in that cold it would not even be pushed. Just in time we raced to the highway ourselves to catch the last bus, which took us far enough into town to connect with streetcars. It was many hours later before husbands had located wives and rescued or joined them. What a night – but forever memorable.

In 1944 gas was strictly rationed. My allowance would take me to Scarborough and back from the Beach, but

not to school, and certainly not down to the coast painting. I was hungry for the Gaspé. Through the Red Cross
nurse whom I had met there in 1941, we were able to
borrow a house, and Virginia and I took off by train for
a month of hard work. Our house was next door to the
Red Cross station, with Lillian Baird, the nurse, and
Elaine, her assistant, ready to be our friends and our
liaison with the resources of fresh lobster, fish, vegetables,
and homemade pies of the district. The Kennedys and
Curry arrived by car a week later and settled into cabins
not far away.

On our first day out, Ginny and I were arrested by the
military police for sketching near the railway bridge. We
protested that we had made a proper application to Ottawa to be allowed to paint on the coast, that we had a
telegram at the house granting permission and that we
were highly respectable citizens, well known in our home
town of Toronto. None of that was accepted. A telegram
had no identifiable signature. We were bundled into a
jeep and driven the thirty or so miles up the coast to Gaspé
village, to the military headquarters for the district. There
we were immured in Colonel Pineau's office and left alone
to cool our heels for a couple of hours, while someone
attempted to reach the right office or person in Ottawa.
We found it amusing to be closeted with all the maps and
official papers. It was almost a pity not to be a spy.

I was working in oils that summer, as I usually did in
those days, and for the first time tackled some on-the-spot
canvases. I had made a train-worthy crate with slots to
keep the paintings apart, and I found it exhilarating to
move beyond the small panels.

Ginny and I prepared dinner for the seven of us quite

often. Lillian's vegetable garden and her freezer provided generously. We were glad to contribute labour. For one such occasion Ginny offered to make a chocolate cake. But there were no matching cake tins for the upper and lower layers. One pan was deep, the other really a shallow pie tin. No matter. And of course we were using the oven of a woodstove with no thermostatic control. No matter. When the cake began to smell tempting, we peeked and saw that the thin layer was already too brown on the edges. I jerked it out and couldn't stop it sailing out of its shallow tin and skidding across the kitchen floor. Horrors. We pulled the second, deeper cake out carefully, and tipped it onto the wire rack for cooling. But it was far from baked and began to drain right through the rack into the pan that I hastily held underneath. Fortunately, the guests had not yet arrived.

"Delicious" was their word for the dessert, a sector of crisp cake (apparently none the worse for wear) with a soft chocolate . . . pudding? sauce? mistake poured over it.

We had our first experience of Bonaventure Island, the bird sanctuary that lies a few miles offshore from Percé. I have been back many times. It is addictive. We would be landed on the near shore and walk the four miles through the woods to the far side, where ledges of the high stone cliffs were full of nesting gannets. We sat in the grass, just back from their nests, surrounded by the pulsing clatter of the birds that were like wheeling planes overhead, a sound too rhythmic to be noise and too harsh to be music. Close up, the gannets are clean sculptured forms with sharply designed colouring and malignant eyes, with silly ungainly white babies.

We watched the domestic ritual, the return of the hunter to the mate on duty at the nest, the presentation of the offering of seaweed, and the mutual neck-stretching and neck-stroking, and bowing to each other over and over again.

It was on the Gaspé coast that I began the analysis of form that has stood me in good stead ever since. Drawing the changing ribs of a boat, both the ones I could see and the ones that were hidden, gave me a trustworthy contour of hull and gunwale. I learned the lesson that I drilled into my students from then on, that the relationships must be understood before they can be drawn, that form follows function and what you don't see is as important as what you do. I used sometimes to give a student something to hold in his hands behind his back, and expect him to draw it without ever seeing it. A good exercise.

That autumn Lillian Baird came to visit me and was so excited by my cottage on the bluffs that she determined to build herself a cabin beside the sea at Barachois. Once more I was drawing plans, measuring furniture, living imaginatively in it. For Christmas I made her a weather-vane of a Gaspé fishing boat to go on the gable, and by the next summer the last details of her dream cabin were completed, and Ginny and I were the lucky first residents. I felt as if my beloved Fool's Paradise had had a child.

18

Peace

THE WAR ENDED. After the first heart-leap of relief I began to realize that with its end came also the end of the sense of common purpose. There had been positive elements in our life in wartime: the relinquishment of self-serving materialism, willingness to make routine sacrifices for the common good even if these sacrifices were minor for us stay-at-homes. We would soon lose the will to do with less, to trust the government, to postpone dissent. Already the political parties were warming up for the struggle for power. But to me personally, it would also mean the return of the war artists and the probability that Charlie Goldhamer would take back all the senior painting classes, and I would be demoted to teaching the lower grades again.

The end of the war also meant that I could begin to hope for electric power at Fool's Paradise and everything that would follow: an oil furnace, hot and cold running

water, and permanent residence. My original house plans
had not included a cellar, but having become a gardener
I needed one for storage, and I decided to put a huge
cistern in it so that I could forget my balky well and use
rain as my water supply. The ground-level utility room
could become a delightful bedroom if I cut a big window
in it looking towards the ravine. Behind the kitchen I
would add a studio-workshop over the cellar, and a garage behind that. I still didn't know whether I was building a dream home to share with some future beloved or a
spinster's retreat. I kept my plans open for a wing to
accommodate my hopes and in the meantime began
working on phase two.

There were no contractors to be found. I drew up my
plans to scale and managed to get them passed by the
Scarborough building department. It was a great moment
when I posted my work permit on the cottage. I had
decided to be my own builder and to look for local
tradesmen to do the difficult technical jobs. The man who
agreed to dig the foundation and pour the concrete was
either a fool or a crook. I still don't know which. He
caused me endless grief with his shoddy work, but, after
he had done his worst in the early spring while I was still
at school, I had honest workmen and it was a great
summer. I located a good Scottish carpenter who agreed
to come on Saturdays. My right arm was suffering from
overwork (too many buckets of earth and too much
gardening) and could no longer hammer heavy nails, but
the carpenter knew a man who was not long out of
hospital, and who therefore couldn't lift weights, but
could hammer. With a seventh of a carpenter and my
half-man, as I labelled Syd Alexander, the addition was

framed up on the concrete foundations, sheathed, roofed, and made ready for the plumber and sheet-metal workers. Syd and I worked steadily and amiably all week and waited eagerly for words of praise when the carpenter saw what we had accomplished. "Mm-hmm" was the most we ever got from him. He cut the first rafter for us to use as a pattern, made sure that our bracing was sound, and hung the doors and windows. I spent an hour or two every night cleaning up the site to be ready for the construction work the next day.

With the hill and winter roads in mind, I bought a war-surplus jeep, ideal for chasing around after the building materials that were increasingly hard to find, and adequate to take me back and forth to school once term had started again. It had no second seat, but a box with a cushion on it served any passenger, and I got used to putting out an arm to keep him or her from falling off when I turned a corner. I taught Virginia Luz to drive, and at her test, the examiner objected to the method of signalling turns that she was using. Since the side windows were fixed pieces of plexiglass, I had taught her to use my system of holding a hand up at the back window and gesturing right or left to warn the car behind. The examiner insisted on conventional hand signals, which meant removing the side panels completely, and Ginny still suspects that her success in the test was partly due to the way the wind caught her full skirt from time to time and sent it billowing up around her neck.

Dawson Kennedy once sent me a postcard addressed to "The Girl with the Jeep, Scarborough," and it reached me in better time than many a letter today. But my fondest memory of the jeep was the summer night that Walter

and I went dancing at the Royal York Hotel. Walt's
second marriage had ended in estrangement and divorce,
and he was once more in attendance. Walt was in summer
white and I in my bridesmaid pink chiffon. I drove up to
the hotel and handed the jeep to the astonished parking
attendant. When we came out hours later, he greeted us
with, "Your car is the second in the far row." "Aren't you
wonderful to remember where everyone is parked?" I
said, which gave him his best laugh of the day.

My fears about my postwar timetable were justified,
and Peter would listen to none of my pleas. He avoided
me when making up the complex charts on which he
sorted out teachers, classes, and rooms, using Ginny as
his assistant. She did her best for me, but Peter was
stubborn. I used to lie awake on June nights when the
schema for next year had been decided, fighting my
resentment and sense of injustice. I was the most active
painter on the staff and had been handling senior classes
with success, but in Peter's mind I seemed still to be
identified with the timetable that I had inherited from
Edith Manning. Ginny had come on the staff ten years
later than I but had walked into Nory's pattern of senior
classes at once. I found this hard to bear.

Late in the Forties, Florence Smedley, witty, beautiful,
passionate Florence Smedley, moved up from Saint-Lambert in Quebec and settled at the Beach, attracted by the
fellowship she had found at St. Aidan's. She had been a
teacher of English at Montreal High School and had been
much involved in the Student Christian Movement and
left-wing politics in Montreal. At one of Dr. Sharman's

Bible study camps in Algonquin Park she had met Nancy
Caudle and they had become friends. While visiting
Nancy later in Toronto, Florence was introduced by her
to Dr. English, and the two had the kind of explosive
argument that neither could forget. The exchange of
books and letters that followed was the beginning of a
deep and lasting friendship. It was an important factor in
Flo's decision to move up to Toronto and join us at St.
Aidan's.

After the war and the lifting of gasoline rationing, Nan
and Flo and I planned a painting trip in the jeep down to
Quebec. Peter gave me the name of a good pension at
Cap-à-l'Aigle, and we booked ourselves in for a few
weeks in July. I discovered that our dates there coincided
with Bobs' and Peter's, and I was appalled. The last thing
I needed in the holidays was more of the same. But to
change plans at that point would have been too obvious,
so we decided to accept the inevitable and make the best
of it.

Those weeks with the Haworths were a turning point
in all our lives. Peter and Bobs made us warmly welcome
the night we arrived and took us out in their car to show
us the best spots for sketching. The next day as I was
coming up the hill to the door laden with my gear, Peter
opened it for me. I was stunned, and began to feel like a
woman instead of a bootboy. In response to his changed
attitude, I softened and relaxed, and we began to enjoy
each other. Peter and Bobs seemed to take it for granted
that we would all go together to paint and share the picnic
lunches that were packed for us. Every day became a
party. Both Flo and Nancy charmed and stimulated the
Haworths, and I could hardly believe that this was the

petty tyrant I worked for at school. One night, shortly after Flo and Nan and I were in bed, we discovered a bat flying around the room. True to my newfound role of helpless female, I cried out for Peter. I thoroughly enjoyed the mad ten minutes of lamplit noise and confusion as Peter rushed about in his pyjamas to rout the little creature and rescue his three maidens from peril.

Flo was an amateur among professional artists, but eager to play around with the paints she had brought. Her work was primitive and inspired. Nan and I were so impressed that we avoided giving her any instruction, feeling that her instincts were taking her farther than we could have led her. The daisy field she painted had every daisy in it ready to pick. One of us did suggest to her that day that the sky was perhaps too pale, and we watched between fascination and horror as she used the dirty water that had not quite drained from her box to darken it. Nan and I looked at each other and said no more.

I disliked my own work that summer. Flo's imaginative fumblings made me feel that my sketches were pedestrian, competent but boring. Bobs had always had magic in her painting. I struggled on with my honest, tedious landscapes, but I was yearning for a change of impetus and direction.

I found it a year later. Back at CTS we had an influx of veterans who were granted an opportunity by the government to get the education they had missed by going into the armed forces. For many it was a valuable second chance, a path into the careers they had been denied by the Depression. Most of the students in these rehabilita-

tion classes were men, but there was also Smitty, a stocky
WAC sergeant, who could, and occasionally did, lay a large
man on his back. She stood for no nonsense, and there
was plenty of it among the rehabs. Most of the time they
worked hard, but one day, horsing about in the life room,
one of the boys managed to dislocate his shoulder and
ended with his arm twisted up around his neck. No
matter. He was loaded, with some difficulty, into a car
and taken off to the Western Hospital, which had a
standing arrangement with the school to care for our
casualties.

These veterans had seen action in the war and now
were back in a school with an administration that was
geared to secondary school students. Anyone missing the
nine o'clock bell was expected to call at the vice-
principal's offices to pick up a late slip, which would
admit him to class, and was further expected to serve a
detention after school. One day my class of rehabs were
slugging away at still life in concentrated silence. There
was a shattering crash. I marvel that those shell-condi-
tioned men did not dive under the tables. The lad who
had been kept waiting for ten precious minutes in a
line-up outside the vice-principal's office had expressed
his rage and frustration by raising one of the big wooden
drawing-boards over his head and slamming it down with
all his strength on the heavy oak table.

The rehab classes restored Dino Rigolo to us. He had
come to the department early in the war, a young Italian
immigrant, sweet, merry, very talented, with sideburns
that made him look like a gigolo. Half-way through his
second year with us, while still technically an enemy alien,
he was drafted into the army. On one of his leaves he came

back to visit us, in khaki shorts, sideburns gone, his hair
brush-cut, as sweet and merry as ever, and so attractive
that I could hardly keep my hands off him. He returned
as a rehab and was outstanding even in that good group.
When Dawson Kennedy took a sabbatical leave the next
year Peter took Dino in as his replacement, and every
Grade Nine and Grade Ten girl in the department fell
madly in love with him. He went on to the National Film
Board, and he well deserved the Canada Fellowship for
overseas study he won there. Another gift of the rehabs'
program was that they crowded the department to the
point that I was needed for advanced classes and at long
last had a satisfying timetable.

After the years of restricted travel, I was hungry for
the sea. Virginia's mother's illness was keeping her on
duty at home, and Peter and Bobs were in England when
I took off in the jeep with Jimmy and Del Thorne to the
place on the Atlantic coast closest to Toronto. This turned
out to be Rockport in Maine. After a week there, grateful
for the smell of the ocean and all the familiar trivia of a
fishing village, we visited Gloucester, a few miles farther
south. It was full of artists and art schools. We called in
to see the Romano studio, with its dozen or so students
working from a model. I came out somewhat drunk on
colour and paint, and determined to throw caution into
the tidal pools.

This was the beginning of what I now call my post-Ro-
mano period. I began working with primary colours, raw
or lightly stirred together rather than mixed, using black
paint joyfully and without regard for realism, letting pure
white separate the forms and act as a foil to the colour.
This was fun!

The next summer Peter and Bobs drove me down to
the Gaspé, and I had the satisfaction of introducing them
to wonderful Barachois and even to Bonaventure Island.
That July, and off and on for twelve years afterwards, we
stayed at Mrs. Jean's. Liza and Willie Jean were Jersey
Island stock like many of the coastal families, English-
speaking with a French lilt. Liza's sister, Ceci, came down
from Montreal on her holiday to help out with the visitors. Meals were beautiful, served on china that had come
over with Liza as a bride. The lunches they packed for us
were works of art. The Kennedys, who had originally
discovered the Jeans, joined us that first summer and
often afterwards. Flo and Nan came in later years, Virginia usually, other friends from time to time and family
occasionally. The Jeans' guest-book has the names of
many artists and their friends scattered through the
pages.

When Peggy Aiken was there with Don Neddeau, she
and I would start the morning with an ocean dip, running
across the lawn and the road to the beach and straight
into the water. To hesitate was to be lost. The sea had been
full of ice floes a few weeks before and it was paralysingly
cold. As soon as the momentum of the run was exhausted
we ran back out as fast as we could, gasping for breath.
Then the glow started.

After breakfast the cars were packed and we took off,
sometimes in separate directions, sometimes together.
Lunch was always social, eaten among the cod-heads and
fishing gear on the dock or huddled out of the wind beside
a shed or a beached boat. We used huge umbrellas to give
us shade for working, guyed three ways with ropes held
by stones or driftwood. Twice a day, as the tide changed,

the wind shifted and the ropes needed to be adjusted or
the umbrellas moved to follow the sun. You would see
someone up, struggling with the ropes, and one after
another of us would follow the lead.

The hour of day we all looked forward to and shared
was tot time. We gathered in Willie Jean's tool shed,
which he allowed us to use as a studio, with the day's work
pinned up or leaning against the wall. The faint smell of
fish, old wood, and gasoline was part of the charm. Then,
drink in hand, we approved, or tried to approve, or
questioned. By the end of the second drink, candour was
apt to overcome tact. I held my breath to hear what Bobs
would say about my painting because I cared more for
her opinion than for all the others'. She never flattered,
and her silence spoke volumes to me. When she praised,
my spirits soared. And I learned from studying her work.
Knowing her subjects, I could appreciate the twists of
perception, the puckish humour, the lovely personal colour that she used.

All winter the monthly meetings of the Ontario Society
of Artists continued this experience of being an artist
among artists. In those days the society received an
annual grant of $3,000 from the Department of Educa-
tion and worked hard at educational projects across the
province. A feature of the annual juried show was the
special section for which twenty or thirty of the artists
each painted a picture based on a theme chosen by the
society or constructed a large didactic panel illustrating
some principle of colour or composition. At the annual
exhibition in the Toronto Art Gallery, the section was
hung in a separate room, and afterwards it was sent off
on tour to galleries, schools, and colleges across the

province. As a member, I was committed to producing
something each year for this section. I saw my work in
relation to the senior artists, L.A.C. Panton, A.J. Casson,
and all the others, and was reassured to feel that it stood
up well.

I had never stopped trying to see Mother, calling at the
Balsam Avenue home and having the door closed in my
face. Mrs. McGill told me when Mother sold the house
and moved to a bungalow in Birch Cliff just east of the
city. I called there too. She usually opened the door to my
knock, said, "What do you want? I have nothing to say
to you," and closed it. But shortly after the end of the war
I made one more of these painful attempts. This time she
said, "Do you want to come in?" We had a polite formal
call of about ten minutes. I went again soon, and again,
and again, the calls getting longer and easier. I was invited
to share the meal she served to Aunt Mabel and Uncle
Charlie when they came up from Montreal to see her. But
she would never come to Fool's Paradise.

Never – until the summer of 1949, when Cousin
Florrie and Dotty, Grandfather's niece from Lévis, were
coming out to spend the day with me. They were both of
Mother's generation and I urged her to help me entertain
them. Since she could feel herself giving rather than
receiving, she graciously consented. I called for the three
ladies and drove them out. Fool's Paradise was lovely
with the garden in its August bloom. Lunch was served
on the porch, and we sat afterwards in the shade of the
big tree on the lawn, Mother working on one of her

cutwork tablecloths while we talked. I carried afternoon tea out there.

When I excused myself to start making dinner, Mother asked if she could help, and I was so glad of the co-operative atmosphere, so unwilling to say no to anything she suggested, that I said, "Yes, thank you very much," and asked her to pick me some ripe tomatoes from the garden behind the house. As Mother carried them out of the bright sunshine into the comparative gloom of the studio, she failed to see the cellar stairs just inside the door, stepped back, and tumbled down the steps into the cellar, breaking her back.

The doctor whom I called refused to come. "Get an ambulance and take her to the hospital." I called an ambulance, called Doug, and left Cousin Florrie and Dotty gossiping on the lawn in comfortable ignorance until help had arrived. Mother was in great pain and had to be lifted out of the cellar on a stretcher, with no room to turn it at the top of the steps. That process was the substance of nightmare.

The ultimate irony of the accident was that I was the one who received the most sympathy. To have this happen the first time she was ever at my home! Perhaps there was irony also in the way my weeks of daily attendance at the hospital dissolved the barriers between us and took us into a new phase of our relationship. I wrote on September 9, 1949: "Mother was walking unaided this afternoon, and for the first time managed to get from lying to sitting without assistance. These weeks of every day at the hospital have been strangely rewarding, and I've missed Mother very positively on my Saturday off and

these first two days of school when I didn't get down to
St. Mike's till late afternoon." Mother had a tremendous
will to recover her mobility and independence. She en-
dured the pain of the therapy with dogged courage and
made rapid progress. My friends rallied and visited her
in hospital and then at home. Marjorie lived a couple of
blocks away and dropped in often with home-made bread
or cookies. Roy was wonderful with her, doing the man's
chores that she found for him. Neighbours enjoyed coming, for she could be entertaining and amusing when she
chose. From then on, Mother accepted me as her daughter, her confidante, her support.

Virginia's mother died as school began that fall, ending
two years of a courageous fight with cancer. One day that
autumn, we were together down in the teachers' lounge
talking about the future. I suggested that we were both
due for sabbatical leave, but that her long ordeal with
Jessie Luz gave her priority. Did she want to take next
year off? If not, I did, and would apply to Peter, but she
had a right to first chance, and I would wait for her to
decide. We don't remember who first said, "Wouldn't it
be great if we could go together?" The minute the words
were spoken we were on fire.

Peter said, "It would be all right with me, but the
principal would never let two people go out of one department."

"May we ask him?"

Down we went to the principal's office and put our
question to Graham Gore.

"It would be all right with me, if Peter would let you

go, but the director of education wouldn't release two of you at the same time."

"Do you mind if we ask him?"

We were able to make an appointment for that same day, and down we went to College Street to see the Big Boss. When we went into Archie Morgan's office, the sun behind him was shining through his ears, turning them vermilion. It is a permanent image. Before he answered us, he filled his pipe, lit it, put his feet up on the desk, and took a great pull.

"I think it's a hell of a good idea," he said. "You'll have a much better time together."

A few weeks later, January introduced the year – 1950 – I was to turn forty, and every cliché about life beginning then seemed to be true. I was no longer self-conscious about my failure to marry. Instead I had accepted my status as a single woman and discovered that there were rich consolations. Most of my near friends were in happy marriages, but I was too close to them not to observe the compromises and sacrifices by which they earned that happiness. They paid the price willingly and would not have changed places with me for the world, but I was beginning to realize that I didn't want to trade places either. By this time I had all the children my heart had room for, theirs and many I had acquired on my own. I was glad not to be part of the diaper-and-formula conversations at one end of the room, much preferring to discuss furnaces with the men at the other. In the art community I was at home with both men and women, content with friendship and no longer yearning for ro-mance.

The long struggle to grow up and be an adult, not only

in my own mind but in Mother's, was over. Mother's six years of ostracism had given me six years of independence in which I had found fulfilment as a woman and some confidence as an artist. I had become a happy teacher, secure in my relationship with my students, giving them riches that I had had to dig deep to find for myself. I was no longer afraid of being outshone by my own students. Their brilliance was my delight and I knew the excitement of drawing out of them their best work and of watching them go on past me to further fields of achievement.

I had my own home in a setting that seemed to me close to perfection. The saplings that Madeline Bennett had helped me plant were becoming trees, the shrubs were spreading to fill the gaps, and the borders were full of bloom. My two cats, Nicky and Tammy, had rabbits to chase, pheasants to fly up in their faces, a fox to come around after dark and bark improper proposals to them, a life of such freedom that I envied them and longed for the day when I too would be able to enjoy Fool's Paradise even on weekdays.

My salary as a teacher allowed me to paint whether or not I made sales. I could pay my taxes, buy my supplies and frames, and live carefully but comfortably, without extravagance but without money worries. I could afford painting trips and the theatre. I was even able to feel well-dressed thanks to a shop at the Beach where I could depend on finding clothes that fitted my disciplined figure and suited my taste and budget. Part of my understanding of my job in those days was that as a teacher I must look like a lady, complete with hat and gloves on the street. It amused me to be dressed up formally in my jeep.

What I still wanted badly and was willing to strive towards with all my dedication and energy was growth as an artist. I knew no magic formula for this. Every Thanksgiving or Easter at Haliburton was a new challenge that I approached in fear and hope. I realize now how dependent I am on response from others for my own judgement about my work, and it was to be a few more years yet before I was given the public recognition that would build my confidence and let me enjoy the results as well as the process of being a painter.

In the meantime I was heart-free and rich in friends. Marjorie was closest of course, the one person who had always believed in my work as well as in me. She would be Mother's daughter while I was away so that I could go with an easy mind. And when some well-wishers, on hearing of the plans for overseas, said, "You'll meet some nice man," my laughter was genuine. I had what I wanted as a woman and now I had also the prospect of a whole year to explore new horizons as a full-time artist. Was this not happiness?

This book was typeset by Tony Gordon Limited in Cochin, a typeface that originated with the Peignot Foundry in Paris about 1915. It is based on the lettering of eighteenth-century French copperplate engravers. In America, Monotype adapted it in 1917, followed by ATF in 1925. Today it is available both in photo-typesetting and as an Adobe face. The roman is distinctive but the italic even more so, being closer to formal handwriting or engraving than most italics.

Book design by Linda Gustafson

Printed on acid-free paper by D.W. Friesen & Sons Limited